Pitseolak: Pictures out of my life

ᐱᓯᐅᓚᒃ: ᐅᓂᒃᑖᐊᒃ ᐃᓅᓯᐅᑕᐅᑐᒥᒃ

© Dorothy Eber, 1971
First paperback edition, 1978
ISBN-0-19-540297-9
Library of Congress catalog card number: 72-4111

Design:
Rolf Harder and Ernst Roch
Printing:
Gazette Canadian Printing Ltd.
Typesetting:
Metro Typesetters Inc. (English)
Department of Indian Affairs and Northern Development (Eskimo)
Printed in Canada
234-098

The drawing 'A bird for the doctor' is reproduced with the kind
permission of Dr. and Mrs. Samuel Adams.

Pitseolak:
Pictures out of my life

ᐱᓯᐅᓚᒃ
ᐅᓂᒃᑑᐊᒃ ᐃᓄᓯᐅᑕᐅᑐᒥᒃ

Edited from tape-recorded interviews by Dorothy Eber

ᑕᓇ ᓂᐱᓕᐅᕈᑎᔾᒃ - ᓂᐱᓕᐊᒡᒐᐅᔪᓂ ᑕᒡᒍᓪ ᐊᒃ ᓇᔾᒃ
ᓄᒪᓂ ᓚᔾᓇᐊᒍ ᐅᓂᒃᒪᓚᒃᓚᒃ ᐊᒍᐊᓚᒃᐊᒍ ᔾᓚᐅᔪᒃ

Published by
Design Collaborative Books, Montreal
in association with
Oxford University Press, Toronto

ᐅᒡᓄᒪ ᐊᒃᑕᐅᔾ
Design Collaborative Books, Montreal
ᐃᒃᔾᓂᒃᔾ
Oxford University Press, Toronto

Acknowledgments

The publishers wish to express their appreciation and
thanks to
The Department of Indian Affairs and Northern Development for provision of the Eskimo text,
The Canada Council for a grant to assist with the tape-
recording,
The West Baffin Eskimo Co-operative for its loan of stone
cuts, engravings and original drawings,
The National Museum of Man for its loan of stone cuts and
engravings,
Mrs. Alma Houston for advice and encouragement.

ᑲᐅᔭᓂᕐᒍᔭᏁᒐ

ᑕᒡᐊ ᐊᑐᐊᓚᒪᐅᑐᒍᑦ ᐃᓄᒃᑎᐱᑐᓂ ᓇᑯᒪᒍᓚᖑ ᐃᓄ
ᐱᓇᕆᐊᑎᕐᑲ ᐃᓄᑎᑕᒪᑎᐱᒡᐅᒪᑕ ᑕᓕᒐᒪᓚ,
ᐊᒪᓗ ᐊᕐᕆᑕ ᓂᐱᐊᑐᓂᔪᑦ ᐃᑲᕇᑲᐅᐃ,
ᑲᒪᐊᓯᒪᐅᓗ ᑯᐅᐊᕿᒪ ᑎᑎᕐᓰᑲᐅᐱᓐᒪᓂᕐᖃᐅᑲ ᐊᑐᓂᕇᑲᐅᒍᑦ,
ᑲᓇᑕᒪ ᒪ ᓄᑕᐅᕆᔪᓂ ᕿᒪᐱᐊᑲ ᑎᑎᕐᓰᑲᐅᐱᓐᒪᓂᕐᖃᐅᑲ
ᐊᑐᓂᕇᑲᐅᒍᑦ,
ᐊᒪᓗ ᐊᓂᒪ ᕇᐱᒐ ᐃᓚᐃᓚᒐᓰᐊ ᑲᓄᓚᐅ ᐱᒐᐱᓐᓚᒐᓗ,
ᑕᒡᐊ ᐃᓄᓇᑎᕐ ᐊᕐᒐᓚᒍ ᓇᒍᒥᑕᐅᒐᑦ.

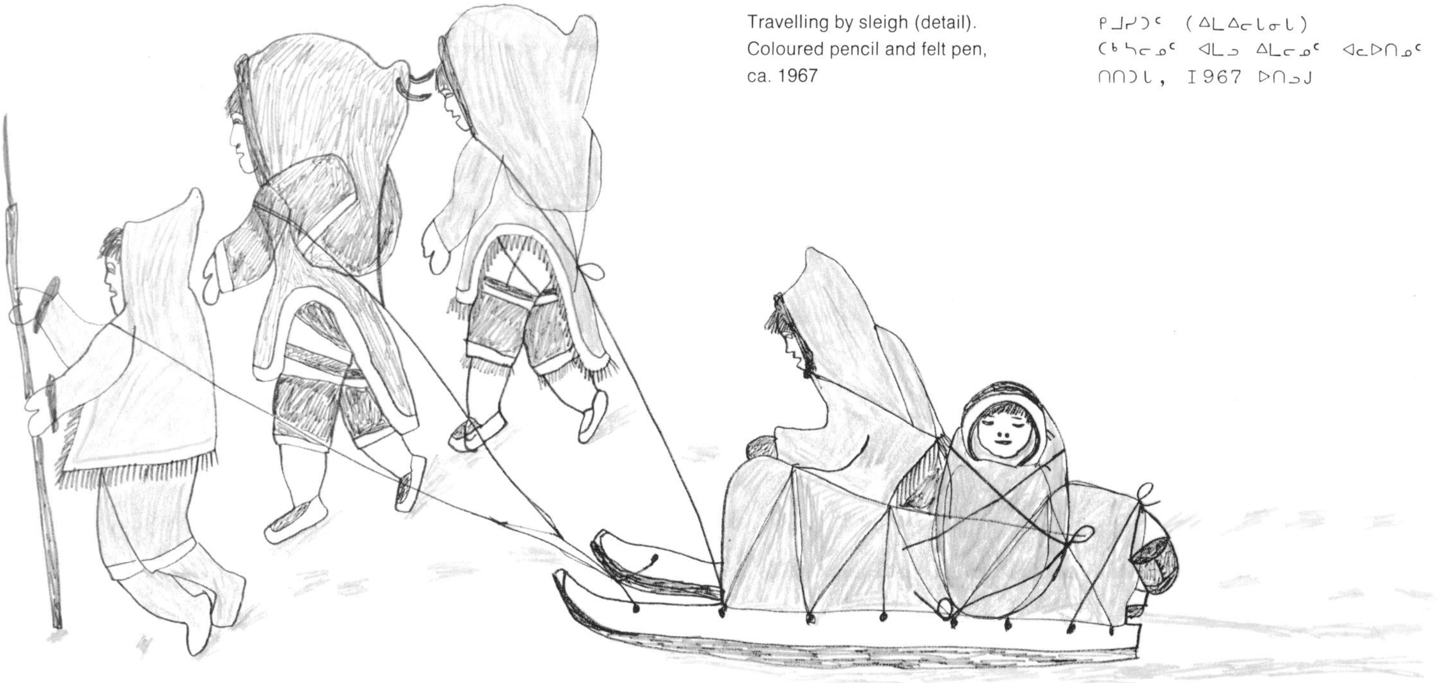

Travelling by sleigh (detail).
Coloured pencil and felt pen,
ca. 1967

ᑭᒧᓯᑦ (ᐃᒪᐃᓕᒐᓂᒐ)
ᑕᒃᓴᓕᖕᑦ ᐊᒪᓗ ᐃᒪᓕᖕᑦ ᐊᓚᐅᑎᖕᑦ
ᑎᑎᑐᒐ, I967 ᐅᑎᓗᒍ

Foreword

It is mid-July, 1970, and brilliant Arctic summer, when I ask Pitseolak if I may tape her autobiography. I have come to Cape Dorset on Baffin Island especially for the purpose and, very soon after the Nordair Otter touches down, I go looking for Quatsia Ottochie. Quatsia, nineteen and a modern Eskimo beauty, knows at firsthand the story of the Cape Dorset art movement. Her father, Ottochie (whose name she has adopted now that Eskimos need surnames), has worked in the craft shop of the West Baffin Eskimo Co-operative since shortly after print-making began, in the late fifties. Her English has been perfected by a typing course in the south, and she agrees to interpret and help put my proposition to Pitseolak. So, with tape recorder, a big bag of tapes, notebooks and coloured pens and drawing paper, we present ourselves at Pitseolak's house. At the beginning of the sixties most Baffin Island Eskimos still lived on the land in igloos and skin tents but now, like Pitseolak, they live in clapboard bungalows.

ᑲᐅᔭᑎᓯᐅᑎᒋᑦ

ᔪᓗ ᑕᑭᒐᓂ, I970-ᒥ ᐊᒪᓗ ᑲᐅᒪᔪᐸᓗᑎᓗᒍ ᐃᓄᐃᑦ ᓄᓇᒐ ᐊᐆᔭᑯ, ᐊᐱᓯᓚᐅᔪᔪᒐ ᐱᓯᐅᓚᒥ ᓂᐱᓕᐅᕈᓇᒪᒐᒪ ᐅᓂᑲᐅᓯᓚᐊᒐᓂ. ᑭᒐᓄᓚᐅᑐᒐ ᐃᓄᐃ ᓄᓇᒐᓄ ᑕᓯᒥᒐᓗᐊᒍᐊ ᒍᑎᑲᓯᒐ; ᐊᒪᓗ ᑲᒐᑕᓯ ᑐᕆᕋᒍᑐᐊᒪ, ᒥᕕᒧ ᑕᓇ ᐃᓄᐃ ᒪᓂᑲᓴᑕᕕᓂᒐ ᓄᓇᒥ ᒪᓂᕋᒥ ᑲᑲᐃᑦ ᐅᒐᑕᓂ ᓄᓇᓕᓂᑦ ᒪᑐᐃᒪᔪᓂ, ᑭᓂᓯᓚᐅᑐᒐ ᑯᐊᓯᐊ ᐅᒃᑐᑭᒥ. ᑯᐊᓯᐊ I9-ᓂ ᐅᑭᐅᑲᑐᒃ ᐊᒃᓇᓯᐊᐸᐅᓗᓂ, ᑲᐅᔭᒪᓴᐅᑎᕆᓚᐅᑐ ᓯᕗᓕᒥ ᐅᓂᑲᑐᐊᒐᓂ ᑭᒐᐃᑦ ᓴᓇᒍᐊᑲᑕᓂᕆᓂ. ᑯᐊᓯᐊᑉ ᐊᑕᑕᒐ, ᐅᒃᑐᑭ (ᑕᓯᒪ ᐊᑎᒐ ᑯᐊᓯᐊᑉ ᑎᒍᐊᒍᒐᒥ ᒪᓇ ᐃᓄᐃᑦ ᐊᑎᑲᑎᐊᑲᒪᑕ), ᐃᑲᓇᐃᔭᓯᒪᓕᑐ ᓴᓇᒍᐊᓯᒪᔪᑯᕕᒥ ᐃᓄᐃᑦ ᓄᓇᒐᑕ ᑯᐅᐊᐸᒐᓂ ᐱᕆᐊᓯᕋᑕᑎᓗᕆᑦ ᑎᑎᑐᔭᓕᐅᓯᔪᕕᓂᒃ, ᐊᕋᒍᐃ I950 ᐱᕆᐊᓯᒪᓕᑎᓗᕆ. ᑯᐊᓯᐊ ᑲᓗᓇᑎᑐᓯᐊᕈᓇᓚ ᐅᑐᒃ ᐃᓕᓂᐊᓯᒪᒐᒥ ᑎᑎᕋᐅᑎᒥ ᓇᑭᑕᑐᒥ ᑲᓗᓇᑦ ᓄᓇᒐᓂ, ᐊᒪᓗ ᐊᕆᓚᐅᑐ ᑐᓴᕈᐅᕆᐊᓴᒥᓂ ᐃᑲᔪᓗᓂ ᐅᑲᐅᓯᑎᔪᒪᔭᓂ ᐱᓯᐅᓚᒧ. ᑕᐃᒪ ᓂᐱᓕᐅᕈᑎᐅᑉ ᓂᐱᓴᕆᓂ ᐃᐱᐊᔪ ᑕᑕᓗᒍ, ᐊᒪᓗ ᑎᑎᑐᔭᕕᓴᓂ ᐊᕈᕆᕆᑐᓂᓗ ᑎᑎᕋᐅᑎᓂ ᐊᒪᓗ ᐸᐃᐸᓂ ᑎᑎᑐᔭᕕᓴᓂ ᓇᔭᓯᓯᓄ ᐃᑎᓕᓚᐅᑐᒍ ᐱᓯᐅᓚᑉ ᐃᒃᓗᓕᓄ. ᐱᕆᐊᒐᑕᑎᓗᕆ ᐊᕋᒍᐃ I960 ᐃᓗᓇᑲᓴᑎ ᐃᓄᐃ ᓄᓇᒐᓂᒥᐅ

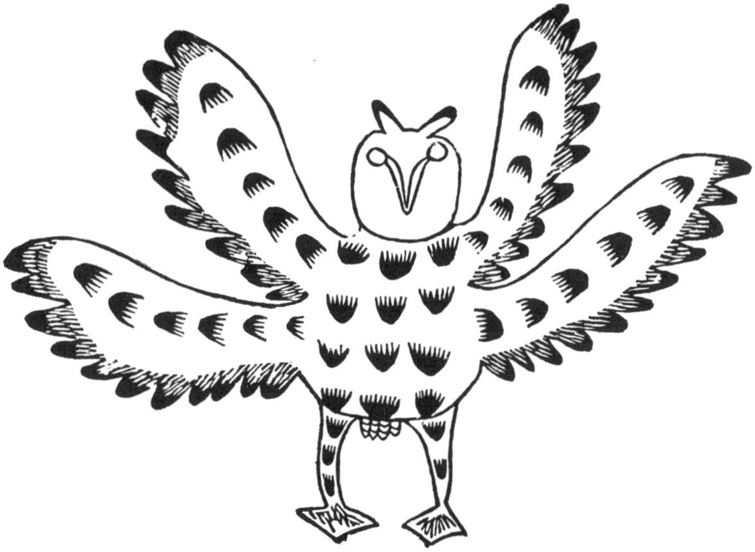

Bird.
Stone cut, 1967

ᑯᐸᓄᐊᒃ
ᐅᔭᕋᒥ ᑎᑎᑐᒐ, 1967

Pitseolak and I have met two years earlier and, with the help of Quatsia, we exchange greetings. Quatsia and I take off our rubber boots and walk into Pitseolak's warm kitchen. Quickly I realize that since our first meeting "acculturation", as the sociologists say, has proceeded at a speedy clip. Then, Pitseolak sat on the floor and drew as we talked; now she sits on a couch, there is a telephone on the wall and across the room is a bowl of plastic flowers. But there is soon no doubt that Pitseolak herself is the same: wise, humorous, a sage commentator on the sociology of change and, of course, the possessor of a remarkable talent which allows her to draw as many as six pictures a morning of vivid interest and beauty.

After preliminaries, Quatsia explains there are people in the south who would like to make a book with some of Pitseolak's drawings and prints and her life story, told in her own words. There is brisk talk back and forth and then Quatsia says, "She doesn't mind to do it but she is getting old now. She is getting kind of shaky and the drawings

ᓯᓕ ᓄᓇᒥᓚᐅᑐ ᐃᒃ ᓗᕕᒐᒥᓯᑎ ᑭᓯᓂᓗ ᑐᐱᒃᓯᑎ ᒪᓇᓕ, ᐱᓯᐅᓚᑎᑐᑦ, ᐃᒃ ᓗᑐᐃᓇᒥ ᐃᒃ ᓗᑲᓕᑐᑦ.

ᐱᓯᐅᓚᓗ ᑲᑎᒋᐅᓚᐅᓯᒪᔪᒍ ᐅᑭᐅ ᒪᕈ ᓇᓯᒪᓕᑐᒃ ᐊᒪᓗ, ᐃᑲᔪᑎᑲᒥᓯᒐᑕᐅᒃ ᑯᐊᓯᐊᒥᒃ, ᐅᑲᑲᑎᒋᓯᑕ. ᑯᐊᓯᐊᓗ ᑲᒥᓚᓯᓄ ᓂᑭᓕᐅᕕᒐᓄ ᐅᑯᔪᒧ ᐃᑎᑐᒍ. ᑲᐅᐴᓴᐅᑎᒋᐊᐱᑐᒐ ᑕᐃᒪᒐᓂ ᑲᑎᓚᐅᓯᒪᒐᑯ ᓯᕗᓕᒥ "ᐃᓄᐃ ᐃᓄᓯᑐᑲᕕᓂᒐᓂᒃ" ᑲᐅᐴᓴᑎᒃ ᐅᑲᐅᓯᑎᓯᒪᔭᒐᑎᑐ, ᓯᑲᑐᐸᓗᒥ ᐊᐴᐅᒋᓕᓯᒪᔪ. ᑕᐃᒪ ᐱᓯᐅᓚ ᐃᓯᕙᓗᓂ ᓇᑎᒥ ᑎᑎᑐᔭᓯᓯᓂᓗ ᐅᑲᑎᓗᑕ; ᒪᓇᓕ ᐃᓯᕙᐅᑕᓗᒥ ᐃᓯᕙᓕᑐ, ᐅᑲᓚᐅᑎ ᐊᑭᓇᒥᓗᓂ ᐊᒪᓗ ᐃᒃ ᓗᒍᓯᐅ ᑐᑭᐊᓂ ᐳᒍᑕ ᓄᓇᒍᐊᑕᑲᓗᓂ. ᐃᓚ ᓯᐊᕈᓕᒪ ᓇᓗᓇᒋᑐᒃ ᐱᓯᐅᓚ ᑕᓇᓴᐃᓇᐅᒋᐊᒐ: ᓯᓚᑐᓗᓂ, ᑯᕕᐊᓯᑐᐃ ᓇᓗᓂ, ᐃᓯᒪᓯᐊᓗᓂ, ᑲᐅᐴᒪᓯᐊᑐ ᐃᓄᐃᑦ ᓄᓇᒐᑕ ᐊᐴᐅᒋ ᓕᓂᒐᓂᒃ ᐊᒪᓗ, ᓯᑲᐃᒪ ᐊᑭᓯᐃᐴᒃ, ᐊᔪᒋᓂᒥᓄᑦ ᑕᐃᒪᓇ ᑎᑎᑐᔭᓗᓂ ᐅᓄᓂᑲᑐᓂᒃ ᐱᒐᓯᔪᑐᓂ ᐊᐴᒍᐊᓕᐅᓗᓂ ᐅᒃᓚᑯ ᐃᓄᓯᓚᑎᑎᑐᑦ ᐱᐅᔪᐸᓗᓂᒃ ᐃᓇᑯᓇᓗᑎᓗ.

ᐅᑲᑲᑎᒋᓚᐅᓯᑕ ᑲᓄᐃᓂᒋᓂᐊᑕᑎᓂ ᑯᐊᓯᐊ ᑐᑭᓯᑎᓯᓯᐊᓚᐅᑐ ᑲᓗᓇᑦ ᓄᓇᒐᓂᑐᓂᒃ ᓴᓇᔪᑲᒍᒪᒪᑦ ᐅᓂᑲᑐᐊᒥᒃ ᐱᓯᐅᓚᑉ ᑎᑎᑐᔭᑕᕕᓂᒋᓂᒃ ᐊᒪᓗ ᐃᓄᓯᒐᑕ ᐅᓂᑲᐅᓯᒐᓂ, ᐅᑲᓯᒪᔪᓂ

Joyful owl.
Stone cut, 1961

ᑯᐱᐊᕐᒐᑐᖅ ᐅᒃ ᐱᖃ

ᐅᖕᕐᒥ ᑎᑎᑐᒪ, 1961

are sometimes shaky. And she doesn't remember everything though she remembers many things.''

All is arranged. For the next three weeks I spend nearly
every afternoon at Pitseolak's house. There are frequent
interruptions to these taping sessions. There are telephone calls, and Pitseolak's grown-up children and her
grandchildren often come in to listen or to visit. One day
a son brings ice cream tubs, the greatest treat of the year.
They have arrived that day on the long awaited sea-lift.
He also brings molasses which Pitseolak says is to put in
the tea. ''I used to like it in the camps and I still like it,''
she says. All conversation stops while these good things
are relished.

Each day, when I arrive, Pitseolak brings out a large
sketch book and we look at the drawings she has done
in the morning — they are rarely shaky and always they
show Pitseolak's distinctive line and style. Then we
move on to reminiscences. Pitseolak's memories do not

ᓇᒥᓂ ᐅᖃᐅᓯᖕᒥ ᐊᑐᓄ. ᓯᖃᑐᒥ ᐅᖃᖃᖕᑐᖃᓄ ᑕᐊᒪ
ᖁᐊᔪᐊᖅ ᐅᖃᓄ "ᑕᐊᒍ ᑲᐊᓯᖅᑐᖅ ᐅᓄᖃᐊᑕᐅᖃᐊᒍᓄ
ᑭᐊᓄᒍ ᒪᓇ ᓂᕐᐅᔅᑕᐊᑐᖅ. ᓴᐊᐊᒍᐊᑕᓄ
ᑎᑎᑐᑕᒥ ᐃᓄᓄ ᓴᐊᓄᔅᑕ. ᐊᒪᓄ ᐊᐅᑕᐊᕐᑐᒪᑕᖅ
ᐃᓄᓂᖕᑕ ᐊᕐᓄᖅ ᐊᐅᑕᐊᒪᓄᐊᕐᓄ".

ᐃᓄᒥ ᐊᖅᕐᒪᑕᓄ. ᐱᓄᐊᕐᒥᓂ ᐱᒪᕐᓂ ᑭᓄᖑᐊᑕᒪᖅᒃ
ᐱᕐᐅᑲ ᐊᕐᖑᓄᖅᑲᓄᐅᑐᒪ. ᖃᖃᑐᕐᖃᖃᑎᓄᒍ ᑕᐊᓄᒪ
ᓂᐱᓄᑐᓄᑕ. ᐅᖃᑕᐅᑎᓄ ᕐᓄᖃᖅᑲᓄ, ᐊᒪᓄ ᐱᕐᐅᑲ
ᑭᑐᒥᓂ ᐃᓇᐅᑲᐊᔅ ᐊᒍᑕᕐᓄ ᐊᑎᕐᓄᖕᖅ ᖃᓄᐊᑐᕐᑎᖕ
ᑐᓄᑎᐊᑐᑕᓄ. ᐊᑕᐅᕐᐱᐊᕐᓄ ᐊᖅᓄᒪ ᑎᕐᐅᕐᐊᑕᕐᑕ ᐊᒍᓄ
ᖁᐊᖅ, ᑕᓇ ᐊᕐᓄᕐᒡᖅ ᐱᓄᑎᑐᑐᕐᑕ ᐊᕐᒍᒻᒥ. ᑕᐊᐊ
ᑎᑭᓄᑐᕐ ᑕᐊᕐᒪᓄᐅᑐᒍ ᐊᑐᓄ ᑐᑭᐱᕐᑐᕐᑎ ᕐᑐᕐᓄᒪᓄ.
ᐊᒪᑕᐅ ᑕᓇ ᐊᖅᓄᒪ ᑎᕐᐅᕐᐊᑕᕐᑕᕐᖅᖅ ᒪᓄᓴᕐᕐ ᐱᕐᐅᑲ
ᐅᖃᓄ ᑎᒍᒡᖅ ᐊᓄᕐᒪ. "ᒪᒪᑎᕐᑲᐊᑐᕐᖅᒥ ᖃᓇᓂᕐᒡᑕ ᕐᑕ
ᒪᒪᑎᕐᓂᒥ". ᐅᖃᓄ ᐱᕐᐅᑲ. ᐊᖅ ᓄᐊᑎ ᐅᖃᖃᑎᑐ ᖃᖃᑎ
ᑕᐊᐊ ᒪᒪᑐᐊᔅ ᓂᑎᕐᐅᓂᕐᒪ.

ᑲᐅᑕᓄᔅ, ᑎᑭᑕᒪ, ᐱᕐᐅᑲ ᓄᐊᕐᓄᒍ ᐊᕐᕐᓄ ᑎᑎᑐᕐᐱᕐᓄ
ᑭᕐᓄᑕᕐᒍ ᑎᑎᑐᕐᐱᕐᒪᒃᓄ ᐱᕐᐅᑲ ᑎᑎᑐᕐᑕᕐᐱᕐᓂᕐᒪ ᐅᑕᒍ--

usually concern the hunt or the harsh times many Eskimos experienced in the old days. Many of the hours we spend together are 'how-to' sessions – how to sew a sealskin tent, how to make mukluks, how to catch a goose without a weapon. She also speaks of domestic felicity and home-life in the camps. In fact, when Pitseolak speaks of difficulties, they are usually the ones the new times have brought along. Like people of the older generations all over the world, she often worries about her grandchildren and whether they can make their way in today's world.

But Pitseolak's story is also an account of how Cape Dorset, a remote point on the Hudson Strait, became an internationally recognized artists' colony. (Today there is hardly a European or North American public art gallery without a Dorset graphic.) Pitseolak makes mention of many of the Dorset artists; and she also speaks with great affection of two white men: the almost legendary James Houston, now an executive with Steuben Glass, New York, who during the fifties was the first civil administrator for

ᖂᑐᐃᓂᐅᐱᐊᑐ ᑕᐊᐃᐧᑲᒪᖁ ᑕᑯᖑᐳᓄ ᐱᑌᐧᑕᒐ ᑎᑎᕋᓕᑕ
ᐅᑭᓓᐊᑲᕆ ᐊᑭᐧᓓᖂᕋᖁ. ᑕᐊᒪ ᐃᑯᐅᒪᓯᕋ ᐊᕆᐊᐧᖁᑕ.
ᐱᐧᑌᐃ ᐊᐧᑕᒐᕐᕋᖑ ᐊᕆᒪᕐᖃᖀᐧᒪᕋᑐ ᐅᒪᐧᐧᑐᖑᕋ ᐅᖂᖁ
ᐊᖄᕆᖁᑕᐧᑐᒪᖁᖁ ᐊᕐᕋ ᐃᖁᐊᒐ ᐊᑐᕏᒪᕋᖑ ᐅᖀᐧᑕᐧ
ᓕᐧᑐ. ᐊᕐᕋᖀ ᐃᑭᐅᖀᖀ ᑲᓄᒍᑎᕋᐱᐊᑕᔿ ᑲᖁ ᐅᑭᕋᑕᑕ --
ᑭᖁᐊᕐᔾᒪᑐᑕ, ᑭᖁᖂ ᕍᕋᕐᒪᑐᑕ ᖁᕐᐧᐱ ᑭᕐᓕᖁ ᑐᐊᕆ
ᑭᖁᖂ ᑲᕐᖂᐅᕐᔾᒪᑐᑕ ᑭᖁᖂ ᖑᑭᕐᒪᑐᑕ ᖁᖀᐅᑎᕋᑐᒍ.
ᐱᐧᑌᖀ ᐅᑭᐅᕐᑲᖁᑐᕐ ᐃᓕᕋᕋ ᖂᐊᐧᕆᖀᕐᕐ ᐊᑲᖁ
ᐊᖁᖂᕆᓚᖁ ᐃᖁᕐᕐᕐ ᖁᖁᕋᖂᕐᕐ. ᐊᑐᕋᑐᕆ, ᐱᐧᑌᑕᕐ
ᐅᑭᐅᕐᕐᑲᖁᑐᕐ ᐊᑭᐅᕆᖁᕋᖂᖀᓂᖁ, ᑕᑯᐊᖁᑲᑕᑐ ᓚᖁᖁᑐᕆ
ᐊᑐᕐᑲᑐᕆ. ᑕᑯᐧᖑᑐ ᐃᖁᐊᓚ ᐃᖁᑐᖃᖁᖀᕐᕐ ᖁᕐᖂᓓᐊ
ᕆᖂᐧᐊᕆ, ᐱᐧᑌ ᐃᖁᖁ ᐊᕆᒪᖁᖂᑲᖁᑲᑐᖀ ᕄᖁᕆᕋ
ᕐᕋᖁ ᐊᖁ ᐊᑕ ᒍᑕᕆᑕ ᕐᕋᖁ ᐱᔿᖁᖂᐊᖂᖁᕋᖁᖑ ᐱᐅᕆᕋᖁ
ᓚᐅᕆᑕᖀ ᕆᑕᐧᖁᕋ.

ᐃᑕ ᐱᐧᑌᕐ ᐅᖁᑭᐧᖀᖁ ᐅᖁᑲᖂᕐᑲᐅᕆᑕᑐᑕᖁ ᑭᒪᐊᕐ
ᑲᖁᐊᖁᓓᖁ, ᑕᐊᕏᒪᖀᐧᖂᖁᑐ ᐃᖁᐊ ᖁᖁᓚᖁ Hudson Strait
ᕋ, ᑕᖁᖀᕐᖁᒍᕆᖁᓚᕐ ᑎᑎᑐᕐᑲᑕ ᖁᖁᕆ. (ᓚ ᐱᑕᑭᕆᐊᕆ
ᑐᖁ ᐃᑐᑎᕆᕋᑐᖁ ᐅᖂᖁ ᐊᕐᐊᑲᖁᑕ ᖁᖁᑕᑕ ᑕᖁᓚᖁ
ᖁᖁᑕᕐ ᖂᖁᕐᓓᖁᑕᖁ ᑭᕋᖁᕆᐊᓚᖁ ᐱᑕᖂᖁᖑᔾ ᑭᕋᕋᖁᕐ ᑎᑎ

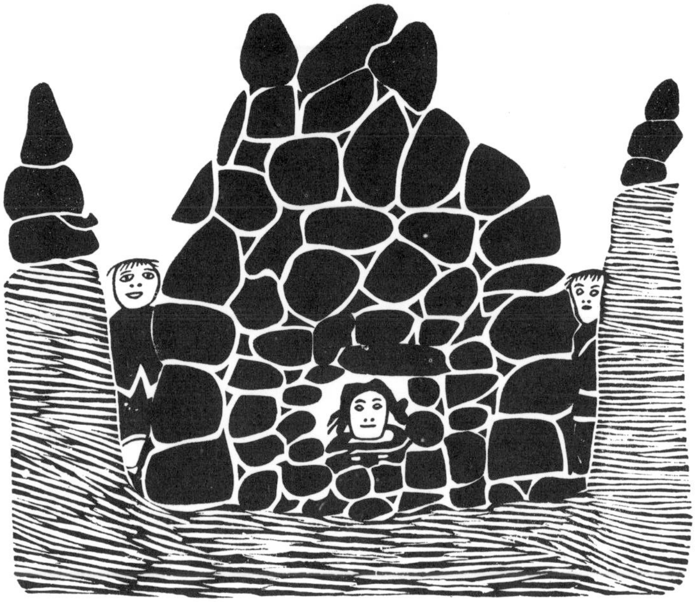

Ancient stone dwelling.
Stone cut, 1966

ᐅᕿᓯᐊᕈᐊᓗᒃ ᐃᓗᕆᔭᐅᕿᑐᕕᓂᒃ
ᐅᔭᕋᒥ ᑎᑎᑐᒐ, 1966

West Baffin Island; and Terrence Ryan, art director of the West Baffin Eskimo Co-operative.

Both have played major roles in the Cape Dorset story. It was James Houston who first encouraged Eskimos to send their carving south. They have a centuries-old tradition of craftsmanship in stone and bone; and in the nineteenth century they sold many small ivory carvings, often with incised drawings, to the crews of the whaling ships. Houston first saw their carvings in the late forties on a sketching trip he made to the North. He brought back examples to the Canadian Guild of Crafts and then, on expeditions he made to camps and settlements, first for the Guild and then as a Canadian government officer, he asked for carvings to sell in the south. He first visited Cape Dorset in 1951 and, perhaps impressed by the talent of the people, from 1957 until 1962 when he left the Arctic, made his headquarters there. In 1957, he and a small group of Dorset artists began their exciting experiments in print-making.

ᑐᔭᒐᕆᓂᒃ). ᐱᓯᐅᓚᒃ ᐅᑲᓚᐅᒥᔪᒃ ᐊᒥᓯᕆᐊᕆᑦ ᑎᑎᑐᔭᑎ ᑭᒐᓂ; ᐊᒪᓗᑕᐅᒃ ᐅᑲᐅᓯᑲᓚᐅᒥᔪ ᐱᐅᕆᔭᓕᐸᓗᓯᓂ ᒪᕈᓂ ᑲᓗᓇᓂ: ᐱᐅᓂᐸᒃ ᐅᑲᓴᒪᑎᓚᐅᑐᒃ ᔭᐃᒥᓯ ᔪᓯᑕᓐ, ᒪᓇ ᐃᑲᓇᐃᔭᓕᑐ ᐊᓕᕈᓕᑎᕗᓂ, ᓂᐅᕈᐊᒃᒥ ᐊᒥᐊᑎᑲᐃ ᓄᓇᒐᓂ, ᐊᕋᒍᐃᑦ 1950 ᐱᕆᐊᒐᑕᑎᓗᕆᑦ ᓯᕗᓕᐸᐅᓯᓂ ᐃᓄᓕᑎᕗᕕᓂ ᐃᓄᐃᑦ ᓄᓇᒐᓂ ᓄᓇᓯᐊᒥ ᐊᒪᓗ ᑎᐅᑎ ᐅᕋᐃᔭᓐ ᓴᓇᒍᐊᒐᓄ ᐊᒐᔪᒃ ᐃᓄᐃᑦ ᓄᓇᒐᑕ ᑯᐅᐊᐸᒐᓂ.

ᑕᑯᐊ ᑕᒪᒥᒃ ᐱᒍᕗᓯᒪᔪ ᐱᕆᐊᑲᓂᐸᒥ ᐱᒍᕗᓯᑎᒃ ᑭᒐᐃᑦ ᐅᓂᑲᑐᐊᒐᓂᒃ. ᔭᐃᒥᓯ ᔪᓯᑕᓐ ᑕᓇ ᓯᕗᓕᐸᒥ ᐱᒍᕗᓯᒪᔪᒃ ᐊᐅᓚᑎᓯᑯᕗᓯᓂ ᓴᓇᐅᒐᓂ ᑲᓗᓇ ᓄᓇᒐᓄ. ᑕᑯᐊ 100-ᓂ ᐊᕋᒍᓂ ᐱᐅᓯᑎᔭᐅᓕᑐ ᐃᑲᓇᐃᔭᓯᑎ ᐅᔭᕋᓂ ᓴᐅᓂᓂᓗ ᐊᒪᓗ ᐊᕋᒍᓂᒃ 19-ᓂ ᓂᐅᕈᑎᑲᓯᒪᓕᑐ ᐊᒥᓯᓂ ᒥᑭᔪᓂ ᑐᒐᓂ ᓴᓇᐅᒐᓂ, ᐃᓕᓂᑯ ᓇᑲᑎᓯᒪᔪᓂ ᑎᑎᑐᒐᓂ, ᓂᐅᕈᑎᑲᓯᑎᒃ ᐅᒥᐊᔪᐊᒥᐅᓄᑦ. ᔪᓯᑕᓐ ᓯᕗᓕᐸᒥ ᑕᑯᕆᐅᓯᒪᔪᒃ ᐃᓄᑉ ᓴᓇᐅᒐᒐᓂ 1940 ᐊᕋᒍᐃ ᐱᕆᐊᓯᒪᓕᑎᓗᕆ ᑎᑎᑐᔭᕕᓴᒥᑐᒥ ᐃᓄᐃᑦ ᓄᓇᒐᓂ. ᐅᑎᑎᓯᓕᓚᐅᑐ ᑕᐃᒪᐃᑐᓂᒃ ᑲᓇᑕᒥᐅᓄᑦ ᓴᓇᒍᐊᒐᓕᑎᕗᐅᓗᓂ ᐊᒪᓗ ᑕᐃᒪ ᐊᐅᓚᐸᓗᐃ ᐃᓄᐃᑦ ᓄᓇᕆᓄ ᐊᒪᓗ ᐃᒃ ᓗᑕᓕᓄᑦ, ᓯᕗᓕᐸᒥ ᐃᑲᔪᓚᐅᓗᓂ ᐊᒪᓗ ᑕᐃᒪ ᑲᓇᑕᒥᐅᓄᑦ ᑲᕿᒪᒥ ᐃᓄᓕᑎᕗᐅᓗᓂ, ᑕᓇ ᐊᐱᑎᓚᐅᑐᒃ

Going after fish (detail).
Felt pen, 1970

ᐃᑲᔫᐊᑐᑦ (ᐃᓚᐃᓕᒪᓗ)
ᐊᓕᓐᒍᑦ ᐊᓕᕗᑎᒍᑦ ᑎᑎᑐᒪ, 1970

Terrence Ryan came later to Cape Dorset. He arrived
in 1960 as a summer art student and remained when the
Eskimos asked him to stay. Under his stewardship the
Co-operative has strengthened and demand and interest
in the Dorset graphics have greatly increased. As a result,
the Co-operative helps sustain the community as Eskimos
move from a hunting culture to the computer age.
Like Pitseolak, many of the artists feel great loyalty to their
'Co-op'. (The Co-operative's headquarters, a small
building in the centre of the community with a dazzling
white, yellow and blue optical colour scheme, is always
crowded with carvers and print-makers bringing in their
work and, like artists everywhere, looking quite critically
at the work of others!) As art director, Ryan, who doubles
as the area's justice of the peace, has made it his policy
to restrict his influence and, in assessing the accomplish-
ment of the print-making years, he says, "Perhaps for
the long term the great achievement has been in saving
a record of what the Dorset people have been able
to say graphically at this time."

ᓴᐅᐱᒪᑲᒪᒪ ᓂᐅᑐᓐᖓᓂᑦ ᑳᓂᐊᑦ ᓄᐊᓕᓄ. ᑲᓂ ᕐᔭᓕᐊᒥ
ᓂᐅᑐᒥᐊᓕᑎᑎᐅᕐᒪᖕᔨ ᑭᓗᕝ I95I-ᒍᑎᓄᒍ ᐊᓕᔨ, ᐃᓕᑫ
ᐱᐊᕐᑦᑲᐱᕐᔪᐊᓄ ᑯᐅᕝᓗᒥᕗᐱ ᐊᔪᐃ, ᐱᒥᐊᑭᓐᑲ I957-ᒥ
ᔪᑳᓐ I962-ᒥ ᐊᐅᒐᓕ ᓴᐅᒥ ᑭᓚᐊᕗᓂ ᐊᔪᐃ ᓄᐊᓕᓄ,
ᑕᐃᑯᓂᑎᔫᓂ I957-ᒥ ᕈᕐᑲᐋ ᐊᓚᔪ ᐊᑭᔪᖕᑲ ᑭᓕᒥᐅᑦ
ᓴᒍᔪᐊᓐᑦ ᐱᒥᐊᕐᑯᐊᔫᑦ ᑯᐅᕐᓴᕐᑎ ᑎᑎᔪᕐᑳᓂᓕᒥᕐ.

ᑎᑎ ᐅᖕᐋᕝᖀ ᑎᕿᑦᑐᐃᕐᖀᖕ ᕐᐊᕐ ᑭᓚᕗ. ᑎᕿᑯᐅᕐᔨᔾ
I960-ᐅᑎᓄᒍ ᐊᐅᕐᒍᓐᑦ ᑎᑎᑐᕐᒥ ᐊᓄᐊᕐᓄ ᐊᓚᔪ
ᑕᐃᑯᓂᔪ ᐊᓴᕐᓐᑐᐅᐱᔪ ᐊᔫᓂᑦ ᐊᔭᐊᑎᕐᐅᓕᒥ ᑕᐃᑯᓇᔪᕐᐅᔪᐊᓇ
ᓀᓂ. ᔪᐊᕝᓯᐊᕐᐱᓂᔾᐅᖀᓂ ᔪᐅᐊᕐᑭ ᕐᔪᕐᓵᐅᓂ ᐊᓚᔪ
ᐱᔪᕝᒐᐅᕐᒍᑎ ᐃᐅᕐᓭᐅᓕᔭᓄᒍ ᑭᓕᒥ ᑎᑎᑐᖀᕐ ᐊᕐᕈᕝᒐᕐ
ᐊᕐᓕᒍᑎ. ᐊᓴᕐᐅᓕᔨᔫᓕ ᑲᓇ ᔫᐅᐊᕐ ᐊᑭᕈᖕᑦᑐ ᐱᔨᑕᐅᕗᕐ
ᓄᐊᕙᓄ ᐊᔫᐃᑦ ᖀᕐᓭᓗᕐᑦ ᐊᔭᔪᕐᖀᕐᐅᑦ ᐊᐅᕝᓗᐱ ᐊᕝᑎᓄ
ᖀᔫᕐᐱᖕ. ᐊᕐᐋ ᐱᕐᐅᓕᑐᑦ ᐊᕐᐃ ᑎᑎᑐᖀᕐᑦ ᐊᕿᕐᓕᕐᑦ
ᐊᕝᕐᐊᔪ ᐊᖀᕐᓭᐅᑭᐊᓯᕐᓯ ᔪᐅᐊᕝᒐᔫᕐ. (ᑲᓇ ᔪᐅᐊᑕᐅᑦ
ᐊᓚᕐᑲᔪᐊᓕ, ᒥᕐᔫᔪᔪ ᐊᕐᔪ ᓄᐊᓂ ᑭᓐᓕᔪᑎ ᑯᔪᑕᑦᑲᔫᓕ
ᒥᔪᔪᕐᒪᕝ ᔪᕐᑎᒥ ᑐᔫᕐᑎᓄ ᑕᑯᓯᐃᐅᓕ ᑲᓇᓕ ᒥᔪᔪᕐᒪᕝ
ᑕᐊᓕᓂᑫᒥᓕ ᓂᓂᐅᑐᖀ ᓀᔪᔪᑎ ᑎᑎᑐᕐᓄᔪ ᑕᐊᔪᓕ ᐊᕕᐊᓄ
ᐊᓄᐊᔭᑕᒥᓄ ᑭᒥᕐᕈᕐᓯᔪᓄᔪ, ᑕᐊᓕᓯᐃᐊᔪ ᓀᔪᔪᑎ ᑕᐊᓕᐊᓕᑦ

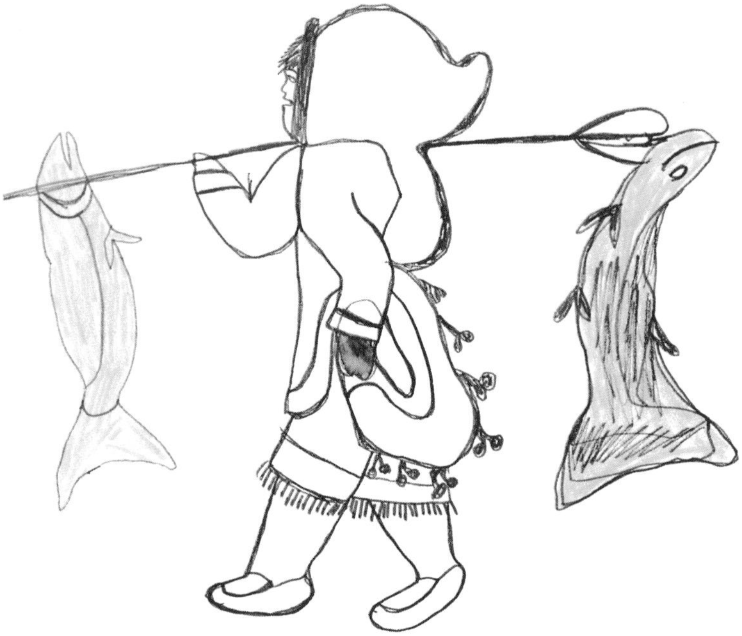

Bringing home the catch.
Coloured pencil and felt pen,
ca. 1967

ᓂᑭᓂᒃ ᐊᓂᕋᐅᔾᔪᒃ
ᑕᒃᓴᓕᖕ ᐊᒪᓗ ᐃᒪᓕᒧᑦ ᐊᓚᐅᑎᖕᑦ
ᑎᑎᑐᒐ, 1967 ᐅᑎᓗᒍ

The first Dorset graphics were offered for sale in 1958 at Ontario's Stratford Festival; each year since has seen an edition of stone cuts, stencils and, after 1962, copper engravings. The Eskimos' radically new style of life means that for the first time they need paychecks and Pitseolak makes no bones about what the prints have meant to her: they have brought her money. But just as emphatically she says they have made her happy. In these difficult times they have provided the sense of pride that goes with work well done.

Readers may notice that in her story Pitseolak never uses dates. Like most Eskimos of her generation, she relates all events to other important happenings – the building of the first Hudson's Bay Company buildings (1913); the sinking of the Hudson's Bay supply ship, the 'Nascopie' (1947); the completion of what in Cape Dorset is known as Pootagook's church (1953). Thus, the white people began to appear in great numbers in the North in the fifties – after the Nascopie went down.

ᓇᒥᑐᐃᓇ, ᓇᑯᑎᔭᑲᓂᓴᐅᓯᑎᒃ ᐃᑲᓇᐃᔭᑕᒥᓂᒃ ᐊᓯᕆᓂ!)
ᐊᒐᔫᒃᑯᓯᓂ ᓴᓇᒍᐊᖕ ᐅᕋᐃᔭᓐ ᐃᒪᐃᑐᕆᐊᓕᓂᐅᔭᕆᑐᒃ,
ᐊᒪᓗ ᐊᑭᐸᓯᓂ ᐊᑭᕆᓂᒃ ᑕᑯᐊ ᐱᓯᐊᓯᕆᑦ ᑕᐃᒪᓇᓯᐊᒃ
ᑎᑎᑐᔭᐃᑦ ᓴᓇᔭᐅᓂᕆᓂᒃ ᐊᕋᒍᓂ, ᐅᑲᓗᓂ ᑕᓇ, "ᐃᒪᑲ
ᐊᑯᓂᐊᓗᒃ ᐃᑲᐅᒪᓇᑐᐸᓗᕕᓂ ᐅᑲᑕᐅᓯᒪᔫᒃ ᐃᑲᐅᒪᒍᑎᕆᓗᕆ
ᑲᖕ ᑭᒐᒥᐅᑦ ᐃᖕᐃᑦ ᐅᑲᒍᓇᓂᒪᒪᒐᑕ ᓴᓇᐅᒐᖕ
ᒪᓇᐅᓕᑐ".

ᑕᑯᐊ ᓯᕗᓕᐸᒥ ᑭᒐᓂ ᓴᓇᐅᒐᐃ ᓂᐅᕈᑎᕆᔭᐅᓚᐅᑐ 1958-
ᒍᑎᓗᒍ ᐊᓐᑎᐅᑏᐅᒥ ᓄᓇᒥ ᐊᕋᒍᑕᒪ ᑕᐃᑲᓂ ᑕᑯᓴᐅᓯᒪ
ᓕᑐ ᐊᑭᓯᒪᓂᕆ ᐅᔭᕋᐃᑦ ᓇᑲᓯᒪᔫ ᑕᓯᑐᐃᒍᑎᓗ, 1962-
ᒍᕆᓯᒪᓕᑎᓗᒍ ᑲᑯᓕᓴᔭ ᐊᔾᓕᐅᕈᑎᕆᓯᒍ. ᐱᓯᐅᓚ ᓯᓇᐅᔫ
ᑏᓯᓗᐊᔭᑏᓇᒍ ᑕᑯᐊ ᑎᑎᑐᕋᐃ ᒥᓴᖕ; ᕿᓇᐅᔭᑕᑎᑕᐅᓚᐅᑐ.
ᐃᓚ ᓂᐱᑐᐃᓇᒥᖕ ᐅᑲᓗᓂ ᑯᕕᐊᓯᑎᑕᐅᓂᒐᓯᓂ. ᐊᑲᐅᒍᓇᐃᑎ
ᓗᒍ ᐃᑲᔫᓯᑲᑕᒪᑕ ᑯᔭᓕᓗᓂ ᐃᑲᓇᐃᔭᓂᒧ ᐱᓯᐊᓯᒪᓗᓂ.

ᐅᑲᓕᒪᑎᑦ ᑲᐅᔾᓚᒐᔫᓴᐅᔫᑦ ᐅᓂᑲᑐᐊᒐᓂᒃ ᐱᓯᐅᓚᒃ, ᑕᑭᒥ
ᐊᑐᓚᐅᓯᒪᔭᕆᒪ ᐅᒃᓗᕆᓂ. ᑕᑯᐊᑎᑐ ᐃᓗᓇᑲᓴᕆᑦ ᐃᖕᐃᑦ
ᕿᒍᓂᑏᔭᕆ, ᐱᓯᐅᓚ ᐃᓚᐅᑎᓯᔫᒃ ᐃᓗᓇᕆᓂ ᐊᑐᑎᔫᕕᓂᓂᒃ
ᐊᓯᕆᓂ ᐱᓗᐊᑐᒥ ᐊᑐᑎᔫᕕᓂᓂ -- ᑕᐃᓇ ᐃᒃ ᓗ ᓯᕗᓕᐸᒥ

The invaders.
Stone cut, 1970

ᐊᕐᖃ ᓴᓂᕙᐃᑦ
ᐅᖅᕐᒥ ᑎᑎᒍᑕ, 1970

Three translators worked on Pitseolak's story. After the first day, Quatsia retired, explaining that she didn't know the Eskimo words for the old things and the old ways. Another young Eskimo woman, Annie Manning, took her place. Annie didn't know all the old words either, but she liked the work. ''It's interesting,'' she remarked, ''finding out about the old way.'' Finally, in order to preserve flavour and nuance as completely as possible, the taped interviews were re-translated word for word by Ann Hanson, justly famous in the Northwest Territories as an interpreter. Related to many of the Cape Dorset people, Ann was born in Lake Harbour and, after her parents died, went to school in Toronto. She translated for the Royal Family during their 1970 visit to Frobisher Bay.

As preparations for the publication of Pitseolak's story proceeded, it was decided that the book should appear in an Eskimo/English edition. The Eskimo text was prepared by Sarah Ekoomiak and Harriet Ruston of the Department of Indian Affairs and Northern Development.

ᓂᐅᐱᐅᑎᑦ ᐃᕐᖃ ᗡᖁᐊᓂᕐᓂ 1913-ᒍᑎᒎ ᕿᐊᕿᐊᒥᕐᖃᐦ ᓂᐅᐱᐅᑎᑦ ᐅᒥᐊᕐᖁᐊᒎᓇᕐᖃ ᓂᐅᐊᕿᕐᓇ ᐅᕐᕿᓂ, ᐊᕐᒍᐱᒥ, 1947-ᒍᑎᔾ ᐱᕐᖁᒍᑎᕐᖃᕐᓂ ᖃᓇᐅᔪᓂᒎᕐᖃᐦ ᕿᒥᕐ ᖃᐅᕐᒪᕐ ᕐᐅᕐᖃᐦ ᗡᒎᔾ ᗡᕿᐊᒪᐃ 1953. ᖃᐦᒪᖃᒎ ᖃᐅᓇᕐ ᐊᕐᒡᕐᖁᖃᐊᕿᕐᓇ ᐃᓄᐃᑦ ᖃᓇᓂ 1950-ᗡᖁᑎᒥ ᐊᖁᒎᐊ -- ᐊᒎᐊ ᐊᕐᕐᖁᐃ ᕿᐊᕿᓇᖃᑎᒎ.

ᐱᓂᕐ ᗡᕐᕐᐊᖃ ᐱᐊᕐᐊᖁᗡᐅ ᐱᕐᗡᖁᐦ ᗡᖁᒃᗡᐊᓇᕐ. ᗡᖃ ᒎᕐ ᕐᕐᖁᖃ ᕿᔾᖃᓇᕐ, ᔾᐊᕐᐊ ᖁᖃᖃᗡᐅ ᗡᖃᒎᕐ ᖃᗡᕐᒪᕿᖃᕐᒎ ᐃᓄᐃᑦ ᗡᖁᖃᗡᕐᕿᕐᖃᐦ ᗡᕿᕐᐊᕿᒎᖃᕐ ᐊᒎᐊ ᐃᖁᕐᒎᖃᕐᖃ. ᐊᕿᕐᖃᖃ ᐃᐊᕐᒎ ᐃᖁᖃ ᐊᕿᖃ, ᐊᕐ ᖃᖃᐦ ᐃᖁᕿᕿᗡᕐᖃᐦ ᔾᐊᕐᐊᕐ. ᐊᕐ ᖃᗡᐊᒎᗡᕿᕐᕿᕿᗡ ᐃᖁᖃᕿᕐ ᗡᖃᗡᕐᕿᖃᕐ ᐃᓇ ᐱᗡᐦᒎᗡᕐ ᐃᖃᖃᐦᓇᕿᕐᖃᐦ. "ᗡᕐᒎᕿᖃᕐᖃ<ᔾᐊᕐᐊᕐ" ᐊᕐ ᖃᖃᗡᕐᖃᐦ "ᖃᗡᐊᕐᕐᕿᕐᕿᐊᕐᕿᕐᖃ ᐃᖁᕿᕐᖁᐦ ᕐᓇᖃᕐ" ᐱᗡᕿ ᕐᖃᖃᕐᖃᗡᐊᕐᖃᐦ, ᐊᕐᕿᕐᖃ ᐊᒎᗡ ᗡᖃᖃᕐᕿᐊᕿᕐᐊᕿᐦ ᐊᕐᐊᕿᗡ ᐊᕐᕿᖃ, ᖃᕿᒎᖃ ᓇᐱᗡᗡᕿᕐᐊᒎᕐᖃ ᐊᐱᖃ ᕿᗡᗡᐊᖃᖃᐦ ᖃᗡᐊᑎᗡᕿᕿᗡᕐᖃᖃᖃᗡᗡᕐ ᗡᖃᖃᖃᕐᕿᕐ ᐊᕐ ᐊᖁᕐᒍ ᐃᖁᖃ ᓇ ᖃᗡᕐᖃᕐᗡᖁᕐᖁᗡ ᐃᖁᐃᑦ ᖃᖃᕿᕐ ᖃᖃᕐᖃᕐ ᗡᕐᐱᗡᕿᐊᒃᐦ. ᐃᖃᖃᒎᕐ ᐊᕿᕿᕐ ᕿᕿᕐᗡᕐ ᐃᖃᕐ, ᐊᕐ ᐃᖃᖃᗡᗡ ᕿᕿᕐ ᐊᒎᐊ ᐊᖃᖃᗡᕿᖃ ᗡᕐᕿᖃᕐᕐᒍᕿᖃ ᐃᖃᕐᐊᕿᖃᗡᗡ ᗡᕐᖃᒎᕐ.

Readers may be interested to know that syllabics,
the phonetic system of writing used by the Eskimos, was
introduced by the missionaries in the late nineteenth
century. Long before schools came to the Eastern Arctic,
nine out of ten Eskimos could read and write in their
own language.

Perhaps, in fact probably, not all the people mentioned in
Pitseolak's account of her extraordinary life will remember
events exactly as she does. But, hopefully, many books
will come out of Cape Dorset. This is Pitseolak's story.

Dorothy Harley Eber
Montreal 1971

ᑕᓇᑕᒪ ᐅᓴᐱᕐᕈᐅᑕᐅᑐᖅ ᐊᑕᓂᐊᖪᑦ ᑯᐊ ᑭᑐᒪᕆ ᓂᐅ
ᕈᕐᒪᑎᖪᕆ ᐃᖃᔮᖪᑦ I970-ᒥ.

ᐊᑐ ᐃᓇᓄᑕᐅᓄ ᓄᑕᓐ ᐊᑐ ᐊᒪᓴᐃᐊᔪᓇᐊᓂᓂ ᐱᕐᐅᑕᑦ
ᐅᓄᑾᐊᓴᐊᓄᕐᓴ, ᐅᑲᑕᐅᕐᓴᐅᑐ ᑕᓇ ᐅᓄᑾᐊ ᐃᓇᓂᑐᓂ
ᒪᕐᐅᑯᐊᒍ ᑲᔪᐊᓂᑦ ᐊᕆᕐᒪᓂ. ᑕᕐᒪ ᐃᓄᑦᓂᑐᓂ
ᓂᑎᓴᕐᒪᓂ ᐊᕆᑕᐅᑐᐅᑐᖅ ᕐᐊᕐ ᐃᐅᒥᐊᖅ ᑲᕐᐊ ᐅᓴᕐᑕᓇ
ᒍ ᐃᓄᓂᕐᐊᖪᓂᒥᐅᓂ.

ᐃᒪᖅ ᐃᓄᓇᕐᐅᑐᕐᖪᑕᓂᑐᖅ ᐃᓄᓂ ᐅᑲᕐᒪᕐᖅ ᐱᕐᐅᑦ
ᐅᑲᐅᕐᖪᕐ ᐃᓄᕐᐅᕐᒪᕐᖪᕐᓂ ᐊᐅᑲᕐᐊᑕᐅᕐ ᑲᓄᕐᐊᖅ ᐱᔪᕐ
ᒪᕐᒪᓂ.ᐃᑦ ᐊᕐᕆᐅᕐᒪᐊᑐᐅᑐᐊ, ᐅᑲᑕᒪᐃ ᑭᒥᓂ ᐱᕐᑐᐃ.
ᑕᓇ ᑕᕆ ᐱᕐᐅᑦ ᐅᓄᑾᐅᑕᒪ.

ᑕᕐ ᕋᐃᕐ ᐃᑕᕐ
ᐊᑭᕐᐊᕐᖅ

Birds of summer.
Engraving, 1964

ᐊᐅᔭᒥ ᑯᐸᓄᐊᑦ
ᐅᑯᓯᓴᔭᒥ ᑎᑎᑐᓚ, 1964

My name is Pitseolak, the Eskimo word for the sea pigeon. When I see pitseolaks over the sea, I say, "There go those lovely birds – that's me, flying!"

I have lost the time when I was born but I am old now – my sons say maybe I am 70. When Ashoona, my husband, died, my sons were not even married. Now they are married and having their children.

I became an artist to earn money but I think I am a real artist. Even when they are out of papers for drawing at the Co-op, they find papers for me. I draw the things I have never seen, the monsters and spirits, and I draw the old ways, the things we did long ago before there were many white men. I don't know how many drawings I have done but more than a thousand. There are many Pitseolaks now – I have signed my name many times.

I was born on Nottingham Island in Hudson's Bay. The year I was born my parents and three brothers began a long

ᐱᓯᐅᓚᒍᕗᒐ ᐊᒪᓗ ᑕᑯᒐᒪ ᐱᓯᐅᓚᓂ ᐃᒪᑯᑐᓂ, ᐅᑲᓗᒐ, "ᐃᑯᐊᑕᒐ ᑯᐸᓄᐊᑯᓗᐃᑦ ᐅᕙᒐᐅᓇ, ᑎᒥᔪᒃ!"

ᐃᑲᐅᒪᒍᓇᒋᑐᒐ ᐃᓚᒐᓂ ᐃᓄᓚᓚᐅᕋᒪ ᐃᓚ ᒪᓇ ᓂᒋᐅᒍᓚᑐᒐ ᐃᒃᓂᒐ ᐅᑲᒪ ᐃᒪᑲ 70-ᓂ ᐅᑭᐅᑲᑐᒐ. ᐊᒃᓯᓇ ᐅᐃᒐ, ᑐᑯᑎᓗᒍ ᐃᒃᓂᑲ ᓄᓚᐊᑲᓚᐅᒋᑐᐃᓗᓂ. ᒪᓇᓚ ᓄᓚᐊᑲᓚᐳᑦ ᐱᐊᕋᑲᓚᓗᑎᓗ.

ᑭᓇᐅᔭᓚᐅᕋᓯᓗᒐ ᑭᓯᐊᓂ ᑎᑎᑐᔭᑎᒍᓚᐅᑐᒐ ᐃᓚ ᐃᓯᒪᔪᒐ ᑎᑎᑐᔭᑎᓗᑐᒋᐊᓴ. ᐸᐃᐸᓂ ᓄᒍᒍᔭᐅᒐᓗᐊᒪᑕ ᑎᑎᑐᔭᕕᓴᓂ ᑯᐅᐊᐸᒥ, ᐅᕙᓄ ᓇᓂᓯᒍᔭᐅᕙᐳᒐ ᑎᑎᑐᔭᐸᑲᒪ ᑭᓯᑐᐃᓇᓂ ᑕᑯᓚᐅᓯᒪᒋᒪᑎᑕᓂ, ᑐᒐᓂ ᐊᒐᑯᓂᓗ, ᐊᒪᓗ ᑎᑎᑐᔭᓗᒐ ᐱᐅᓯᐅᕙᑐᕕᓂᓂᒃ, ᑭᓯᑐᐃᓇᓂᒃ ᐊᑐᐸᓚᐅᑕᑎᓂᒃ ᐅᕙᓯᐊᕈ ᐊᒥᓯᓂᒃ ᑲᓗᓇᑲᓚᐅᑎᓇᒍ. ᑲᐅᐳᒪᒋᑐᒐ ᑲᓯᓂ ᑎᑎᑐᔭᓯᒪᓚ ᒪᒐᒪ ᐃᓚ 1000 ᐅᓄᓂᓴᓂ. ᒪᓇᓚ ᐊᒥᓯᓂ ᐱᓯᐅᓚᑲᓚᑐ ᑎᑎᓯᓯᒪᒐᒪ ᐊᑎᕋᓂ ᐊᒥᓯᕕᓯᒐ.

ᐃᓄᓚᓚᐅᓯᒪᕗᒐ ᑐᔭᓂ ᐃᓄᐃᑦ ᓄᓇᒐᑕ ᑕᕋᓂ. ᑕᓇ ᐊᕋᒍᑎᓗᒍ ᐃᓄᓚᕕᐱᒋᓚᐅᑕᒐ ᐊᑕᑕᑯᑲ ᐊᒪᓗ ᐱᒐᓯᑦ ᐊᓂᑲ ᐊᐅᓚᑎᐊᓯᓚᐅᓯᒪᔪ ᐅᒐᓯᑐᐊᓗᒍ. ᑭᒪᐃᓯᑎ ᓄᓇᒥᓂ ᓴᒃᓗᓂ

Blue insect.
Felt pen, 1970

ᑐᒍᕌᑕᖅ ᖑᐱᑐᖅ
ᐃᐱᓕᒍᑦ ᐊᓴᐅᑎᒍᑦ ᓐᓇᑐᒪ, I970

trip. They left their camp in Sugluk on the coast of Quebec
and set out for Baffin Island to join relatives. They left
in the spring and reached Nottingham Island where I was
born. The next spring they crossed the Hudson Strait
and arrived in the Foxe Peninsula, in the place where Cape
Dorset is today.

But our journey was not quite ended for, the next spring,
we continued along the Hudson Strait and reached
Frobisher Bay. That was when there were no white men
there at all.

These were long journeys and dangerous, too, when the
waters were rough, but I didn't know – I was still being
carried on the back of my mother.

We made all these travels in a sealskin boat. Such boats
had wooden frames that were covered with skins. They
used to be called the women's boats because they were
sewn by the women. Many women sewed to make one

ᑯᐸᐃᒃ ᑐᑭᐊᓂ ᐊᒫᓗ ᓄᓇᑕᓄ ᐃᓄᐃ ᓄᓇᓕᓂ ᓄᓇᕐᐊᒥ
ᑲᓐᕐᓄᓂ ᐃᓭᒥᓂ. ᐊᐅᑕᓛᐅᑐ ᐅᐱᖏᓴᓕᒥ ᐊᐅᓴᓂᒥᓄᓐᖅ
ᐃᓄᐃᑦ ᓄᓇᓕᑦ ᑭᑕᒍ ᐊᒫᓗ ᓐᐱᓄ ᐳᐊᕐ ᐱᓂᐸᓴᑕᒍ ᑕᓇ
ᓄᓇ ᑕᕐᓂ ᑭᓕᐅᓚᖅᕿ ᒪᓇ.

ᐃᓚ ᐊᐅᓯᓂᑎᐅᑕᓲᕆ ᓂᕐᐊᐅᐱᒥᕐᕌᖅ ᐅᐱᓗᓴᐊᕐᒥᒍᕈ,
ᐊᐅᒪᕿᓯᓄᑕ ᐃᓄᐃ ᓄᓇᓕᑦ ᑭᑕᒍ ᐊᒫᓗ ᓐᐱᓄᑕ ᐊᖁᓄᓂᓴ.
ᑕᐊᕐᓕᓂ ᑲᓄᐱᑲᐅᕐᓕᕐᕈᐊᐅᕐᖅ.

ᑕᑯᐊ ᐅᓕᕐᓄᒍ ᐊᐅᓯᓂᑎᐅᑕᓲᕆ ᑲᐱᐊᓄᐅᐊᑐᒥᕐᕈ ᐊᓛᐃᓴ
ᐊᐊᓄᐅᐊᓄᓐᓂᕐ ᐃᓚ ᑲᐅᕐᓕᕐᐅ -- ᕿᓴ ᐊᓗᑕᐅᑕᕐᖃᒪ
ᐊᓄᓄᓄᓴ.

ᑕᑯᐊᓕᓴᓗᕐ ᐊᐅᓯᓂᑎᐅᑕᓲᕆ ᓄᕐᐅᕐ ᑭᓕᓄ ᐅᒥᐊᑲᕐᑕ.
ᑕᐊᓗᐊᓄᕐ ᐅᒥᐊᕐ ᑭᓴᒍ ᐊᑕᑐᑎᑲᓄᓴᓄ ᑭᓴᒍ ᐊᕐᐊᕐᓴᓄ.
ᑕᐊᓴᐅᕐᕿᓴᐅᕐᖃ ᐊᕐᓄᐊᓴ ᐅᒥᐊᓗ ᒥᕿᑕᐅᕐᒪᓕᓄᓴ ᐊᕐᓄᓴᓴ.
ᐊᒥᕿ ᐊᕐᓄᐊᓴ ᒥᕿᕐᐊᓄᐅᑐ ᐊᑕᐅᕐᒥ ᐅᒥᐊᓄᐅᕐᓐ. ᐅᒥᐊᓴ

Mother with child.
Felt pen, 1970

ᐊᖃᓇᖅ ᐱᐊᕐᒧ
ᐃᓚᒐᔪ ᐊᓴᑐᓄᒡ ᑎᑎᒐᒪ, 1970

Crossing the Straits.
Stone cut, 1970

ᐃᖃᑭᒍᑦ
ᐅᖅᖓᒻ ᑎᑎᒐᒪ, 1970

boat. Some boats had sails made from the intestine of the whale, but we had no sail and we had no motors then so my father and brothers rowed all the way. Later, I often heard them say the boat was very full!

But even in my childhood these sealskin boats were already disappearing. My first memory of life is when we stopped in Lake Harbour, on our way back from Frobisher Bay to Cape Dorset, to buy a wooden boat. There were many there. It was while my father bought the wooden boat that I first saw houses and that I saw the first white man. I was scared.

Only as a child was I ever in a sealskin boat, but I have put these boats into my drawings. Perhaps these boats were not really so big but to me, as a child, they seemed very big and I remember them well. I have been drawing the old ways since 'Sowmik' – Jim Houston – came, and many of the drawings have been put on the stone and turned into prints. Did I live all my remembered life in

ᐃᓕᒥ ᑎᒥᖅᐅᑕᖃᖅᐊᑐ ᕿᓪᐅ ᐊᕿᐊᕆᓂᓗ ᕿᕐᐊᓂ ᑎᒥᖅᐅᑕᖃᖅᐊᓄᑦ ᐊᔪᓚᑐᓄᖃᓚᑕ ᑕᐊᒪ ᐊᑐᑕ ᐊᖃᓚ ᖃᐊᑐᑦ ᑐᑕᓕᒪᓚᔪᖅ. ᕐᐊᐅ ᑐᖅᑕᑕ ᐅᖃᑎᒍᕐᑦ ᐅᒥᐊᔪᖅ ᐊᖅᕐᐊᔪᖅ ᑕᑕᑐᖅ !

ᐃᓚ ᐱᐊᕐᐅᑎᓗᓯᓂ ᑕᑯᐊ ᐊᕐᐅᕐ ᕿᒻᕐ ᐅᒥᐊᑦ ᐱᑕᖃ ᔪᓕᑐᐅᑐ. ᕐᐅᑕᕐᒻ ᐊᔪᓚᕐᐅᒪ ᐃᓇᕐᓯᓂ ᐃᒪ ᖃᖅᕐᑕ ᕿᒻᒻ ᐃᖃᔪᓚᕐᕐᑦ ᕿᓚ ᓂᓇᐅᑎᐊᕐᑦ ᕿᕐᐅ ᐅᒥᐊᕐᖅ. ᑕᐊᖃᓂ ᐊᕐᕿᖅᕐᐊᖃᖅᐊᑐᖅ. ᐊᑐᑕ ᐅᒥᐊᑕᖅᑐᓗ ᕿᕐᖅ, ᐅᒥᐊᕐ ᑕᑯᕐᐅᑐᕐᒪᕐᐊᓗ ᐊᓗ ᐊᖅᓂ ᑕᑯᕐᐅᑐᕐᒪᕐᐊᓗ ᑲᓇᖅᒻ ᑕᑯᕐᐅᕐᒻ ᑲᐱᕐᐅᑐᕐᒪᕐᐊᓗ.

ᐱᐊᕐᑐᕐᒪ ᐅᒥᐊᑐᕐᒪᑎᐊᔪᖅᐊᑐᐅᒪ ᓇᕐᐅᕐ ᕿᕐᓂ ᐅᒥᐊᔪ ᐃᓚ ᑕᑯᐊ ᐃᓇᖅᑕᖅ ᑎᑎᑐᕐᓇ. ᐊᓗᖅ ᑕᑯᐊ ᐅᒥᐊᕐ ᐊᕐᕐᐊᖃᕐᐅᕿᑐᖃᐊᕐ ᐊᕐᕐᐊᑐᕐᐊᖃᓂᖅ ᐱᐊᕐᐅᑯᐊᑐᔪ, ᐊᕐᕐᐊᑐᖅᐅᕐᐅᑐᑕ ᑕᐊᒻᖅ ᐊᐅᕐᑕᖅᕐᐊᑐᖅ. ᑎᑎᑐᕐᐅᑐᖅᕐᒪ, ᐅᐸᕐᐊᕐᓄᑕᖅᕐᒻ ᑕᐊᓪᓕᓄᑦ ᖅᐅᒪᖅ -- ᕐᐊᓕᕐ ᐊᕐᑕ -- ᑎᕿᐅᕐᕐᒪᒻ ᐊᓗ ᐊᕐᕐᐊᓗᐃ ᑎᑎᑐᕐᖃᑐ ᐅᕐᖅᔪᑕᕐᐅᕐᐊ ᐊᓗ ᑎᑎᑐᕐᕐᐅᓄᓂᖅ. ᐃᓇᕐᒪ ᐃᓇᓂᕐᐅᑎ ᐊᕐᑎᐅᕐᒪ ᐃᓇᕐᓂᖅ ᕐᐅᕐ ᐱᓄᕐᓇᒻ? ᐊᖃᓇ! ᐊᖃᕐᐊᔪᖅ ᒪᑎᐊᔪᖅ:

Both in summer and winter we used to   ⊲ᗞᔅᒥ ᐅᑭᐅᒥᗜ ᗄᑲᑕᒐ<ᑕᐅᒧᒄ
move a lot.   ᐃᒪᑦᒍ ᐊᑕᐅᑎᒍᑦ ᑎᑎᒐᒪ, I970
Felt pen, 1970

the Foxe Peninsula? 'Ahalona!' . . . Very definitely! And
most of my life I lived in the camps. I remember Cape
Dorset when there weren't any houses. I remember when
they were building the Hudson's Bay post. The same
warehouses that are here now were built when my father
and mother were still alive – when I was just a little girl.

Timungiak was my mother; Ottochie was my father. I had
a happy childhood. I was always healthy and never sick.
I had a large family – three brothers and a sister – and
we were always happy to be together. We lived in the old
Eskimo way. We would pick up and go to different
camps – we were free to move anywhere and we lived in
many camps. Sometimes they were near Cape Dorset and
sometimes they were far away . . . it depended whether
a person wanted to go far or to be near a settlement.
My father hunted in the old way, too – with a bow and
arrow. He had a shotgun but he didn't use it. Sometimes
there were bad winters and we would go hungry but
there was no starvation.

⊲ᒪᑕᐅᑫ ᐃᑭᕐᓯᑕᒪᑫᖕᑫ ᐃᑭᕐᒪᕁᒷ ᑕᒐᑎᓂ ᐃᑲᓄᑫᕋᒧᒥ
ᑕᐃᑲᓂᑕᒪᒍᑫᑕᕁᑕᐅᕐᒡᕁᕈᑕᒣ. ⊲ᐅᑕᕁᕈᕗ ᑭᒪᐃᑕ ᐃᑲᓄᑕ
ᑲᓇᒍ. ⊲ᐅᑕᕁᕈᕗ ᓂᐅᐊᑎᐃ ᐃᑲᔪᓂ ᐃᑲᓄ⊲ᒍᑕᐅᑲᓇᒍ.
ᑕᑫ⊲ᔅᐃᒐᐃᑦ ᑭᒷᑐᐃᒐᑲᐅᑎᐅᕁ ᒪᒐ ᐃᑲᓄ⊲ᒍᑕᐅᕁᕈᕗ
⊲ᑕᑕᒪ ⊲ᒐᒐᓗᕗ ᕐᑕ ᐃᒪᑎᒥ ᑕᒪᒥᕁ -- ᐱᑭᕗᑯᒧᒪ
ᓂᐱ⊲ᕈᕋᒍᑎᓂᒪ.

ᑎᒍᒥᑫᕁ ⊲ᒐᒐᕐᑕᐅᕁᒪᕈᔕ; ᐅᕁᑐᑭ ⊲ᑕᕐᑕᕁᕐᒪᕁᕈ.
ᕁ⊲ᑫᕐᑕᐅᑐᒪ ᐱᒷᑕᐅᕁᒪ. ᑲᓄᐱᕁᒷᕈᒐᓄᒪ ᑲᓄᒪᑕᐅᕁᒪᒥ
ᒍᒪᕗ. ᐃᒪ ᐅᓄᕁᑲᕁᐅᑐᒍ ᐃᕐᕁᕁᑕ ᐱᒪᕈᓂᕁ ⊲ᓂᕁᕗᒪ
⊲ᒪᕗ ᐃᕁᑲᒍᒪ -- ⊲ᒪᕗ ᑕᒪᒪᒪᕐᕁᕁ ᕁᐅⰝ⊲ᕈᕁᑕᐅᒍᑫ
ᑲᓄᒪᕈᑕ. ᐃᓂᕁᐅᒍᒍ ᐃᓂᒪ ᐃᒷᕁᕁᑲᒪᑕ. ⊲ᐅᕁᒐᑲᕁ
ᑕᕁᑕᐅᒍᑫ ᓂᒪ⊲ᒪ ⊲ᒪᕁᕐᒐ ᓂᒪ-- ᐃᕐᒪ⊲ᓂᕁᕁᕁᑕᐅᒍ
ᓂᒪᒍᒪᒪᕁ ᑲᐃᕁᕐᒐ ⊲ᒪᕗ ᑲᐃ<ᕐᒐ ⊲ᕁᕐᕁᒪᕁ ᓂᒪᒪ.
ᐃᕁᓂ ᓂᒪᕈ ᑲᐃᑐᕁ<ᑕᐅᒍ ᑭᒪᒪᕁ ⊲ᒪᕗ ᐃᕁᓂ ᐅᒪᕁᑐᕁ<ᕁᕁᕁ
. . ᕁᕐᕁ⊲ᒪᕁᐃᒪ ᐃᒪᕁ ᐅᒪᕁᕈᕐᒍᒪᕁ< ᐅᕁᕗᓂ ᑲᓄᑐᕐᒍᒪᕁ<
ᐃᕁᕈᕁᑕᒍᕁ. ⊲ᑕᑕᒪ ⊲ᒍᒪᕁ⊲ᕁᕁᕐᑕᐅᑐ ᐅᕁᕈᕐ⊲ᕁᕈᑎᑕᐅ --
ᐱᕁᕈᒍ ᐱᕁᑕᕁᒍᕗ. ᒍᑭᐅᑎᕁᑕᐅᕁᕈᕗ ᐃᕁ ⊲ᑐ<ᑕᐅᒥᕁᑕ.
ᐃᕁᕐᕁᕁᒪᕁ ᐅᑭᐅᕁ ᐱᐅᕁᕁᐅᑐᕁᒍᕁ ᐃᕁᕁᓂᕗ ᑲ<ᕁᕁᐅᕁᑕ ᐃᕁ
ᐱᕁᑐᑲᕁᑕᐅᕁᒪᕗ.

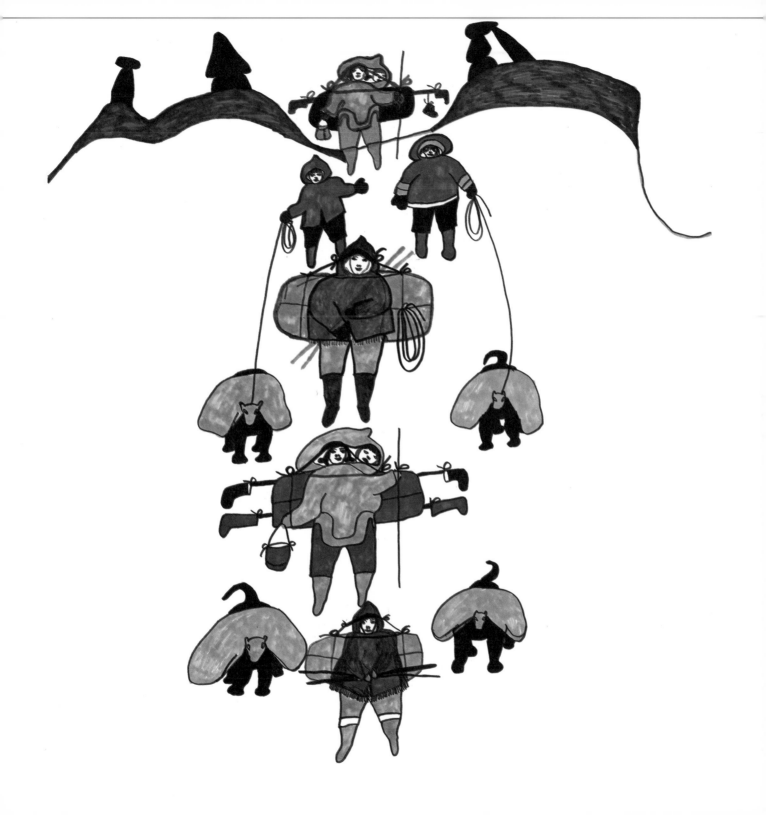

Tattooed woman.
Stone cut, 1963

ᑲᑭᓂᓚᒃ ᐊᒃᓇᒃ
ᐅᔭᕋᒥ ᑎᑎᑐᒐ, I963

In those days many of the women had tattoo marks on their faces and my mother had them, too. They used to do it with a needle and caribou thread soaked in oil and soot from the 'kudlik' – the seal oil lamp. They used to pull the thread through the skin and the skin would be swollen for many days. I don't know exactly why people had tattoos but I believe the women did it because they thought it was pretty. I did, too. When I was young I tried a few marks on my arm, as you can see.

ᑕᐃᓱᒪᓂᐅᑎᓗᒍ ᐊᒃᓇᐃ ᐊᒥᓱ ᑲᑭᓂᑲᐸᓚᐅᑐ ᑕᒃᓱᑐᓱᒪᔭᓂ ᑭᓇᒥᒍ ᐊᓇᓇᒐ ᑕᐃᒪᐃᑐᑲᓚᐅᓱᒪᔭ. ᑕᐃᒪᐃᓗᑐᑎᑲᐸᓚᐅᑐ ᒥᑯᑎᒥ ᑐᑐᑉ ᓗ ᐃᕙᓗᒐᓂ ᐃᕙᓗᑲᓱᑎᑦ ᐅᒃᓱᒥᑎᓱᒍ ᐃᕙᓗ ᑯᓕᓕᓂᑯᒥ ᐸᐅᑲᑎᓗᒍ -- ᑯᓕ ᓇᓱᐅᑉ ᐅᒃᓱᒐᓂ ᐅᒃᓱᓕ. ᐃᕙᓗᒥ ᓄᓱᐃᕙᓚᐅᑐᑦ ᐅᕕᓂᒥᒍ ᐊᒪᓗ ᐅᕕᓂᒐ ᐳᓕᐸᓚᐅᑐᒃ ᐅᒃ ᓗᓂ ᐊᒥᓱᓂ. ᑲᐅᐳᒪᓱᐊᒋᑐᒐ ᑲᓄᓱᐊᒃ ᓱᒧᑦ ᐃᓄᐃᑦ ᑲᑭᓂᑲᐸᓂᒪᒐᑕ ᐃᓚ ᐊᒃᓇᐃ ᑕᐃᒪᐃᓗᑲᑕᑯᑐᕕᓂ ᐃᓇᑯᓇᑐᑎ ᓱᑯᓂᒐᒥ. ᑕᐃᒪᐃᓗᓱᒪᒥᔭᒐ. ᐃᓄᓱᑐᓱᒐ ᐅᑐᕋᓱᐊᓱᒪᔭᒐ ᑕᒃᓱᒐᓱᓱᒐ ᑕᓕᑯᑦ ᑕᑯᒍᓇᐸᑎᑦ ᑕᕙ.

My father used to tell stories about how he was once almost killed by a powerful shaman. My father was a very good hunter and that is why the shaman tried to kill him – he was jealous. I don't know very much about shamans – I don't like to think about them – but my family and my mother's family all believed in shamans because we had heard so many stories. They were Eskimos just like other people but they had these strange powers. They had power over the hunt – they could bring the animals – and they had power to kill. Just as it is today, a long time ago

ᐊᑕᑕᒐ ᐅᓂᑲᑐᐊᐸᓚᐅᑐ ᐅᓂᑲᐅᓱᑲᓱᓂ ᑐᑯᑕᐅᑲᓴᓂᕕᓂᒥᓂ ᐊᑕᐅᓱᐊᓱᓂ ᓱᒍᔭᒧ ᐊᒐᑯᒧ. ᐊᑕᑕᒐ ᐊᒍᓇᓱᐊᓱᑎᐅᕙᓚᐅᑐ ᑕᐃᒪᐃᒪ ᐊᒐᑯᒧ ᑐᑯᑕᐅᒐᓱᐊᓱᒪᔭ ᐊᒐᑯᒧ ᐱᐳᓗᒋᔭᐅᓱᓂ. ᑲᐅᐳᒪᓱᐊᒋᑐᒐ ᐊᒐᑯᐃᑦ ᒥᓴᓄ -- ᐃᓱᒪᒋᔭᒪᒋᑕᑲ -- ᐃᓚ ᐃᓚᑲ ᐊᓇᓇᒪᓗ ᐃᓚᒋ ᐃᓗᓇᑎ ᐅᐱᑎᔭᑲᐸᓚᐅᑐ ᐊᒐᑯᓂ ᑐᓴᓱᒪᒐᑕ ᐊᒥᓱᓂ ᐅᓂᑲᐅᓱᓂ. ᐊᒐᑯᐃ ᐃᓄᑐᐃᓇᐅᕙᓚᐅᒥᔭ ᑕᑯᐊᑎᑐ ᐊᓱᒋᑎᑐ ᐃᓄᐃᑦ ᐃᓚ ᐊᐳᐅᒋᑐᓂ ᓱᒍᓂᑲᐸᓚᐅᑐ. ᓱᒍᓂᑲᐸᓚᐅᑐᑦ ᐊᒐᑯᓂᒥᓄᑦ ᐊᒍᓇᓱᐊᓂᒧ ᐅᒪᔭᓱᐅᓂᒧ -- ᐅᒪᔭᓂ ᓄᐃᑎᓱᒍᓇᓱᑎ -- ᐊᒪᓗ ᓱᒍᓂᑲᓱᑎ ᑐᑯᓱᒋᐊᓴ. ᑕᐃᒪᓴᐃᓇ ᒪᓇᐅᓕᑐᑎᑐ, ᐅᕙᓱᐊᑑ ᓇᑯᑎᐅᑎᒋᑐᐸᓗᕙᑐᕕᓂ

From skins we made buckets
to carry water.
Coloured pencil and felt pen,
ca. 1967

ᑭᓯᔭᓂ ᐃᒥᑕᐅᑎᓴᓕᐅᐸᓚᐅᑐᒍᑦ
ᑕᒃᓴᓕᓄ ᐊᒪᓗ ᐃᒪᓕᒧ ᐊᓚᐅᑎᓄᑦ
ᑎᑎᑐᒐ, 1967 ᐅᑎᓗᒍ

Bird attacking fish.
Coloured pencil and felt pen,
drawing for stone cut, 1969.

ᑯᐸᓄᐊᑦ ᐃᑲᓗᒐᓯᑐᑦ
ᑕᒃᓴᓕᓄᑦ ᐊᒪᓗ ᐃᒪᓕᓄᑦ ᐊᓚᐅᑎᒧᑦ
ᑎᑎᑐᒐ ᑎᑎᑐᔭᑕᐅᑲᓗᓂ ᐅᔭᕋᒥ ᓴᓇᓯ
ᒪᔪᒃ 1969

Composition.
Engraving, 1964

ᐅᑯᕐᒃᕐᒥ ᖃᑉᐅᐊᓐ, 1964

there was often hatred among people. When a shaman was jealous or hated another Eskimo, he would try to kill him and, sometimes, I think, if an Eskimo had an enemy in camp, he would go to a shaman friend and ask him to kill this man who hated him. But they were very good-looking people – you would really never believe they were shamans.

There were good shamans and bad shamans but most people feared them – in the old days there were many things to fear. Some people feared the animals, even the animals they ate. I always feared polar bears – they were scary.

When we were children we played lots of make-believe. We used to play igloo, we used to play dog-team. I think everybody plays these things. Perhaps children every-where play the same things. We played a game in which other children would run after you; if they could catch you they would pretend to eat your eyes.

ᐃᓄᐃᑦ ᐃᓚᓇᑯᑦᒃ. ᐊᒡᑯ ᐃᑦ ᐱᕕᔪᓱᑕᐄᔭᒡᒥ ᐅᕙᔪᓇᑦ
ᐅᒥᕐᑕᒍᐊᒡᒥ ᐃᓄᑲᑎᒥᒃᓄᒃ ᑐᑯᕐᒥᐊᐊᖅᒃᐄᓇᓂᒃ ᐊᒡᒪᔪ ᐃᓚᓇᑯ
ᐃᓄᒃ ᐅᒥᕐᔭᑲᒃᔭᐊᒡᒥ ᓄᐊᓴᓇᑦᒥ, ᐊᒡᑯᔮᒃ ᐊᐊᕐᖴᐅᑦ
ᐱᑲᑎᓇ ᐅᒃᓱᓇ ᑐᑯᕐᑯᒥ ᑖᕐᒥ ᐊᒍᑎᒥ ᐅᒥᕐᕐᖴᓂᒃ.
ᐃᑦ ᑖᕐᐊ ᐃᓇᑕᓇᔭᐊᖅᐄ ᐊᒃᕐᐊᔪ ᐃᓄᐊ ᐅᐱᖴᕐᔭᐊᓇᔪ
ᐊᒡᑯᕐᐊᕐᕐᖴᑦ.

ᐱᐅᕐᓇᒃ ᐊᒡᑯᑲᕐᒃᐊᑦᕐᕐᖴᒃ ᐱᐅᕐᔭᐊᔪᓇᔪ ᐊᒡᑯᑲᔪᓇ ᐃᑦ
ᐃᓇᓚᑲᖴᓂᒃ ᐃᑲᕐᔭᕐᔭᐊᖅᐄᓇᒃ -- ᐅᕐᔭᐊᕐ ᑖᐊᕐᓇᐅᓐᕐ
ᒍ ᐊᕐᕐᓇᒃ ᑭᕐᔪᐃᓇ ᐃᑲ ᕐᐊᔪᒃᐊᑦᐄᒃ. ᐃᑦᕐᒃ ᐃᓄᐃ
ᐊᒃ ᕐᐊᖅᐄ ᐅᓚᕐᓇ ᓂᑦᕐᖴᓇᒃᐃ ᐅᓚᕐᓇ ᐊᒃ ᕐᐊᖅᐄᔪᒃ.
ᑖᐊᒪᓚᒃ ᓇᐊᓇ ᐃᒃ ᕐᐊᕐᐅ. ᓇᐊᔪᔭᐃᒃ ᐃᒃ ᕐᐊᓇᖅᐊᑦᐅᒪᒃ.

ᐱᐃᕐᖴᕐᒃ ᐱᔪᐊᖅᐊᑦᐅᔭ ᐊᕐᕐᓇ ᐅᐱᐊᔪᓇᒥ. ᐱᔪᐊᖅᐊᑦᐅᔪᒃ
ᐊᒃ ᓱᕐᑐᔪᔪᐊᕐᕐᕐᑦ, ᑭᔪᕐᔪᐊᕐᕐᐊᕐᕐᒃᓂᐊ.ᐊᓇᓇᓚᑎᐊ ᐃᓄᐃ
ᑖᒪᖅᒥᓚ ᐱᔪᐊᕐᔪᒃᑐ. ᐃᒪᑲ ᐱᐃᕐᐊᐊ ᓇᕐᑐᐊ ᐱᔪᐊᕐᔪᕐ
ᑖᖅᒥᓚᖴᐊᓇᒃ. ᐱᔪᐊᖅᐊᑦᐅᔪᒃ ᐱᔪᐊᖅᐊᑎᑲᕐᕐᑦ ᐱᐃᕐᖴᑲᐊᑎᓇᓯᒃ
ᐅᓇᑲ ᑖᐅᑎᕐᕐᑦ; ᐊᔪᕐᖅᐅᒃ ᐃᐱᒍᑖᐊᒍ ᐊᒪᓚᕐᕐᑦ.

From my father we used to learn the Eskimo legends. There were many such stories and all children learn them, but I have forgotten most of them now. I remember the one about the blind boy who got back his eyesight when a bird took him on his back and dived with him under the sea three times. This blind young man lived with his mother who was cruel to him and, when he returned home and she saw he could see, this wicked mother was so frightened she jumped into the sea. Eskimos believe she became a white whale and is there still – they really believe it.

There were no teenagers in those days. The young people got married so early they didn't have time to make any trouble. Now there are so many young boys and girls and very often they are troublesome.

The year I married was the year my father died. He had a bad sickness – it was something with the lower back – and he died in our camp at Idjirituq. The year he died,

ᐊᑦᑕᑕᓂᑦ ᑲᐅᐱᖅᐸᓚᑕᐅᐳᒍᑦ ᐃᓄᐃᑦ ᐅᓂᒃᑲᐅᒍᒃᓯᓂᒃ.
ᐊᒥᓱᐊᔪᒃᐸᓚᑕᐅᐳ ᑲᐅᐊᑐᐅᐊᓄ ᐅᓂᒃᐊᑎᓄ ᐊᒪᓗ ᐱᐊᖅᓚᒪ
ᑲᐅᐱᖅᐸᓚᑕᐅᑦᕐᔅ ᐊᓂ ᐳᐊᒍᖨᒪᓄᑲᑉ ᐃᓄᐊᑲᖅᕐᔅ ᒪᓄ.
ᐊᐅᓚᖅᔭᒪ ᑕᐊᒥᕐᒪ ᕐᔅᖨᕐᒥ ᑕᐅᒍᕐᒍᕐᒥ ᑕᐅᒍᐊᓄᐊᖨᓴᓂᒥ
ᒍᓇᔪᖅ ᒍᓄᐊᒍᑉ ᑎᒍᖯᐅᕐᓄ ᐊᒪᒍᑉ ᐱᕐᐸᖨᓂ ᐊᖅᖅᑕᐅ
ᖯᑐᓂᖯᒥ ᑕᐅᒍᐊᓄᑉᐊᖅᓄ. ᑕᓄ ᑕᐅᒍᒥᕐᒍ ᐃᓇᕐᑐ ᖯᐱᖯ
ᐊᓄᓇᕐᓇᕐᐅᓄᐊᖨᓄ ᐊᓄᓇᕐᓄ ᐊᖯᐊᖅ ᖯᕐᓄ ᐊᒪᒍ ᑕᓇ ᖯᐱᖯᖅ
ᐅᓂᖯᐅᐊᓄ ᐊᓄᖯᒍ ᐊᓇᓇᖯᑦ ᑕᖯᖯᑕᐊᓄᒥ ᑕᐅᒍᒍᐊᓇᖨᐊᖯᖩ,
ᑕᓄ ᐊᓇᓇᐅᖯ ᐊᖯᖯᐊᓄᖯ ᖯᐱᖯᕐᖯᕐᒥ ᐊᒥᓇ ᒥᕐᖯᐊᓄᖯ.
ᒪᓄᑕᖯ ᐃᓇᓇ ᐊᒥᕐᖯᐅᖯᐱᖯᖩ ᕐᖯ ᐃᓇᓇ ᐅᐱᖯᖯᐱᐅᖯᖩ.

ᒪᖯᖩᖯᐸᖯᑕᐅᕐᖩ ᑕᐊᖯᒪᖯᐅᖯᖩᒍ. ᒪᖯᖩᐊ ᐃᓄᐊ ᓄᖯᐊᑕᖯᐱ
ᖯᕐᐊᖯᖯᑕᐅᖯᖯᑦ ᐱᒪᖯᐊᓇᖅᖯᐅᖯᖯᕐᖩᐊᑦ ᖯᐊᒍᖯᖯ. ᒪᓄᖯ
ᐊᒥᕐᖯᐊᓄᐊ ᖯᐱᖯ ᓄᐊᖯᖩᐊᓄ ᑕᐊᒪᒪᖯ ᐱᒪᖯᐊᓄᐸᖯᐅ.

ᐊᖯᖩᐅᖩᒍ ᐅᐊᖯᑕᐊᖯᖯᐅᖯᑕᐅ ᐊᑦᑕᒪ ᐅᖯᐊᖯᖯᐅᑕᐊᒥ. ᖯᐅᒪᖯ
ᐸᖯᖩᐅᖯᒪᖯ ᐊᐊ ᖯᐅᒪᖯᐅᖯᒪᒪᖯ ᐅᖯᐱᑕᖯᐊᖯᖯᖯᐅᖯ ᐊᒪᖩ

A drawing out of my mind.
Felt pen, 1970

ᐃᕆᒪᒍᓂ ᓐᓄᑕᕐ
ᐊᓚᓯᒍ ᐊᑕᐅᓄᒍ ᓐᓄᒪ, I970

I remember, there was a ship caught in the freeze-up in the ice just outside our camp. It was a beautiful ship, all white, and owned by Americans. They lived in their ship and the white men spent the time trapping for white fox. They used to send my brothers to the Bay in Cape Dorset to sell the skins and get the money. In the spring when break-up came, after my father died, the ship left.

After my father died, Ashoona's father came to get me on a dog team. Ashoona had told my brothers he would marry me; Ashoona and I used to be little children together. I don't remember how old I was when I married but girls got married very young then; now they are older. Ashoona's father took my mother and me on the dog team to Ikirasaq which is near Sakbuk, a one-day trip from Cape Dorset.

We were married in the summer here in Cape Dorset. At that time of year all kinds of people from all the camps in the area used to come into Cape Dorset to see the ship

ᑐᑯᑕᐅᕐᒪᕋᑉ ᓄᐊᓂ ᐊᑉ ᔅᑯᕐᑐᒥ ᐊᑕᐱᓐᑐᒥ. ᑐᑳᓄᒍ
ᐊᐅᑕᕐᕝᒪ ᐅᒥᐊᕜᐊᑳᓄᒍ ᕐᑯᔫᕐᒥ ᓄᐊᑕ ᓴᓄᐱᑯᔅᓄᓂ.
ᐅᒥᐊᕜᐊᓐᕐᐅᕐᓂ ᐊᒥᐊᓄᑉᕜᐅᓄᑉ. ᐅᒥᐊᕜᓄᓚᐅᕐᕝᒪ ᐊᒪᔪ
ᑳᓄᐊᑦ ᒥᕙᕜᐊᓄᐊᑉᓄᑉᑎᑉ ᓐᓄᒪᐊᓄ ᑳᑕᓕᕐᒥ. ᐊᓄᑐ
ᕐᐅᑉᕙᑕᐅᑐ ᕐᒪᓄᐊᓐᕐᕌᓐ ᓄᐅᒐᓄᕐᐃᐅᐱᔫᕐᓐ ᓐᓄᒪᐊᓄᓄᒥ
ᕐᐊᑐᐅᑐᓐᕜᓄᐊᐅᕐᑦ. ᐅᐱᓐᕐᐅᓄᒍ ᕐᒪᐊᑐᐊᓐᑦ ᐊᓐᕙᓐ
ᑐᑯᓚᓐᒍ, ᐅᒥᐊᕜᐊᑉ ᐊᐅᓚᐅᕐᕝᒪᕐ.

ᐊᓐᕙᒪ ᑐᑯᓚᓐᒍ, ᐊᑉᕐᐊᑉ ᐊᓐᕙᒪᓄ ᐊᑐᕐᐅᑕᐅᕐᕝᒪᕝ
ᕐᒍᕐᐅᑉ. ᐊᑉᕐᐊᑉ ᐅᑉᓄᐅᕐᕝᒪ ᐊᓄᑐᓄ ᐅᕝᓂ ᓄᓄᐊᑕᒍᓚ
ᓄᒪᕐᓂ; ᐊᑉᕐᐊᑉᓄ ᐱᐊᕐᑕᑉᓐᒥᕐᕐᕐᐊᓄᐱᔫᒍ. ᐊᐅᑉᕐᐊᕐᓄᒪ
ᑉᕐᓂ ᐅᕐᐱᐅᑳᓚᒪᒪ ᐅᐊᑕᕙᒪ ᐊᓂ ᓄᐊᑕᕙᐊ ᒪᑐᓚᕐᐅᕐᑕᕐᓂ
ᐅᐊᑦᕐᐊᑉᕝᓐᑦ ᑕᐊᕙᒪᓄ, ᓚᓄᑉ ᐃᐊᓄᓇᕐᕝᕐᐅᑐ. ᐊᑉᕐᐊᑉᓐ
ᐊᓐᕙᒪ ᐊᐊᕐᓄᑕᐅᕐᕝᒪ ᐊᓄᐊᓗᓐᑉ ᐅᕝᓄᓄ ᕐᒍᕝᒍ ᐊᕐᑕᕜᒍ
ᕐᑉ ᕙᐅ ᕐᓂᐊᓄ. ᐅᓴᒥ ᐊᑐᐅᕐᒥ ᐊᕜᕜᐊ ᕐᒪᓄ ᐱᒪᓄ.

ᐅᐊᑦᑕᐅᕐᕝᒪᕝ ᐊᐅᕐᐅᓐᓄᒍ ᑕᓴᓄ ᕐᒪᓄ. ᑕᐊᕜᒪᓄᐱᓐᓄᒍ
ᐊᑕᒍᑉ ᕐᓂᐊᓄᒪᕐᑉᑯᑦ ᐃᐊᐅᑉ ᓄᕐᑐᐊᓂ ᓄᐊᓄ ᐱᔪ ᕐᕙᐊᑉ
ᕙᓄᐊᓄᕜᐱᑦ ᓐᕙᕐᕐᐊᐅᑉᑯᑦ ᕐᒪᓄᑉ ᑕᕐᓄᐊᕐᕐᓐ ᐅᒥᐊᕜᐊᕜᐱ
ᓄᐱᐊᕜᓄᐊ ᐅᕐᒪ ᓄᐱᐊᐊᐱᑉᑦ ᐱᕐᓐᕐᐊᓂ. ᓐᕙᕜᑕ ᐊᕜᕜᓄᐅᕜ

that would bring the supplies to the Bay. When we arrived there were many people camped all over the hill where the Hudson's Bay post is, and all around the bay. We were married outside, by the flagpole near the Bay, by the Anglican clergyman whose Eskimo name is 'Inutaquuq', which means 'a new person'. All the people from the camps were there.

Because Ashoona was an inland hunter, at our wedding I had on caribou skin clothes – but they were just ordinary clothes. Here in the Arctic we did not bother with special dresses. But all through my married life, because Ashoona was such a good hunter, he brought me beautiful skins – all kinds of seal and caribou. Many women used to be jealous of me because I had such lovely clothes.

For a short time after we married, we lived in Ikirasaq but, before my first son was born, we moved to Akudluk Island. It was a long journey but it took us only one day by sail. It was windy and there was a good breeze on

ᒪᕐ ᐃᓄᐃᑦ ᑐᕆᒪᓕᕿᑦᑐᓐ ᓇᒥᑐᐃᓇᒪ ᑲᑲ ᓴᓇᐊ
ᓂᐅᐱᐱᐅᕐᑦ ᐊᕐᑕᖃ ᐊᓚᕐ ᓯᖅᑐᓕᒥᖕ. ᑲᑎᑎᑐᓕᑕᑐᕐᐱᓚᖅᒐᑦ
ᓯᓕᒥ ᓴᐱᓕᖅᑐᓐᑲᐊᒥ ᐃᓚᐅᑦ ᓴᓇᐊᓂ ᐊᖅᑭᑐᐃᐱᔾ ᑲᑎᑎᓇ
ᐅᕐᓇ ᐃᐊᓇᑐᑦ ᐊᑎᑲᑐᑐ ᐃᓇᑕᑲᖕᒥ. ᐃᓇᒪᓕᑦ ᑐᕐᑎᐅᑕ
ᒪᕐᓴᐃ ᑕᐃᑲᓂᑐᑕᑐᑦ. ᐊᖅᕌᓇᖕ ᓇᒥ ᐊᒍᐊᕐᐊᑎᐅᒪᑦ
ᑲᑎᑎᑐᕐᓇ ᑐᑐᕐᓇᖕ ᐊᓇᕐᕈᒪᑐᐱᕈᐊᓪ – – ᐃᓚ ᑐᑐᕐᓇ
ᐊᓇᕐᑐᐊᓇᐅᑐᐱᕈᐊ. ᒪᓇ ᐃᓄᐃᑦ ᓇᓗᓂᒥ ᑲᒪᕐᕌᓚᑕᑐᒍ
ᐊᓇᕐᑐᕐᓇᕐᐊᖅᕐᕿᐊᖅ. ᐃᓚ ᑕᐊᒪᓕᓯᒪ ᐅᐱᐊᓇᓗᓂᒥ ᐊᖅᕐᓇ
ᐊᒍᐊᕐᐊᖅᑎᐅᐸᑐᐱᐅᑐ ᐅᒪᕐᑐᐱᖅᑎᐅᐸᑐᐱᑐ ᖠᕐᕿᐊᒍᓇᖕ
ᐱᐅᐊᓇᖕ ᐱᓐᐸᓇᓗ – – ᑲᐱᐊᑐᑐᐃᐊᓂ ᐊᖅᕐᕈᑎᓂ ᐊᕐᓇ
ᑐᑐᕐᓇᑐ. ᐊᕐᒪ ᐊᕐᓇᐃᑦ ᐱᐱᓴᕐᖕᐸᑐᐱ ᐅᐱᓂ ᐱᐅᕐᐊᖕᓇ
ᐊᓇᕐᖃᖕᐸᑐᒪᒪ.

ᑲᑎᑎᑐᖃᒥᕐᐱᐅᑐᐱ, ᓇᐱᑲᑐᐱᕐᐱᓚᕈ ᐃᐱᕿᖃᕐᒥ ᐃᓚ, ᐊᖕᐱᕈ
ᖃᑎᖕ ᐊᖅᐊᓂᒥ ᐃᐊᓕᓪᑐᐱᓇᒍ, ᓇᓕᐱᕐᐱᓚᕈ ᐊᖅᒍᒡ. ᐊᖃᒍ
ᐊᓯᖅᓕᐱᐅᕐᐱᓚᕈ ᐃᓚ ᐅᖅ ᒍᒥ ᐊᑕᐱᐅᕐᒥ ᖠᕐᕌᖕ ᐅᕐᐊᑐᕐᐱᓕᕈ
ᒪᕈ. ᐊᓇᕐᑐᓇ ᐊᖅᕐᐅᑐᑦ ᖑᕐᑲᑎᖕᒥ. ᐊᐅᓕᐊᕐᒪ

Safe in the tent.
Felt pen, 1970

ᐊᑕᓇᖢᑦ ᑐᐱᒥ

ᐊᒪᓪᒍ ᐊᒐᐅᑎᒍ ᑎᑎᑦᖅ, I970

our necks. I remember it was autumn and it was snowing
but there was no ice on the water. My husband's two
brothers and their families came with us and we were in
camp together for one year at Akudluk.

When Namoonie, my first son, was born, three women
held me. It was like that in the old times — there were
always women who helped. Afterwards, they would make
magic wishes for the child — that a boy should be a good
hunter, that a girl should have long hair, and that the
child should do well at whatever he was doing.

I don't know if it is easier to have babies in a hospital.
Ahalona! At any time it is hard. There is a saying, "It is
hard but it is well." I had 17 children — every year I
had a baby — and many of them died as little children.
In the Eskimo way, two sons were adopted, one by Peter
Pitseolak and one by another Eskimo couple, and
they died, too. Later, a daughter died from having a baby.
My living children are Namoonie, Kaka, Kumwartok,

ᐅᑭᐊᖅᐅᓂᒍ ᖃᓲᓂ ᐃᓐ ᕐᑯᕆᒪᕐᖃᓲᐊᓲᓂ ᐊᒪᖅ. ᐅᐊᒪ
ᓄᖃᒡᕆ ᒪᑭᐊᕐ ᑭᕈᒪᕐᓚ ᒪᓲᑎ ᐅᐸᑎᓂ ᐊᒪᓗ ᑐᐱᕐᒪᖅᑎ
ᕆᓲᑕ ᐊᖃᒍᒥ ᐊᑕᐅᕐᒥ ᐊᑯᓲᒥ. ᓇᐅᒪᐃᐊ, ᐊᒪᕐᕆᐸᖁᑎᒪ
ᐃᓄᒐᓚᐅᕐᖢᕐ, ᐊᖅᓇᓄᑦ ᐱᒪᕐᓇ ᐊᑭᕐᑕᐅᓲᒪ. ᑕᐅᒪᐊᖅ
ᓚᐅᒪᑕ ᐅᕐᕆᐊᖁ -- ᐊᖅᓇᐃ ᑕᐊᒪᒪᑦ ᐊᑭᕐᖃᖅᐅᓲᑦ.
ᐃᓄᖅᕆᒪᒪᒪ ᐊᕐᕆᓇᓚ ᐱᑭᒡᖁᐅᖃᒍᑎ ᐱᐊᓲᒍ ᖃᓇᖅᖃᐅᓲᑎ
ᐊᖅᖃᓚᖅᐅᒍᓚᓂ ᕐᒥᐳᐅᖃᒡᒪ ᐊᒍᐊᕐᐊᕐᓇᐅᕐᖃᐳᓂ,
ᓂᐸᐊᕐᐊᒍᕐ ᖃᖁᒍᑐᕐᖃᐳᒍ ᐊᒪᒍ ᑕᖅ ᐱᐊᒡ ᐱᕐᓇᐅᒪᒍᒍᑦ
ᖃᓇᑐᐊᖃᒪᖅ ᖃᓇᐊᒍᓂᒣᒪᑦ.

ᖃᐅᖁᒪᕆᕐᒍᒪ ᐊᖅᐅᒍᖁᐅᕐᐅᓚᒪ ᐱᐊᖁᒪᑐᐊᖅ ᐊᓇᐊᒥ. ᐊᖅᓇ
ᐊᖅᕐᓚᓲ ᒪᓂᐊᒍ! ᖃᓲᑐᐃᐊ ᐊᖅᐅᓲᑐ. ᐅᐃᒪ ᐅᖃᕐᓚᖃᓲ,
ᐊᖅᐅᓲᑐ ᐃᓐ ᖃᓇᐊᕐᒪᓲ. ᐱᐊᖁᖃᕆᒪᒪᒪ I7-ᓂ
ᐊᕐᓲᒍᑕᖁ ᐱᐊᖁᖃᕐᒪᕐᖃᐅ ᐊᒪᒍ ᑐᓲᕐᒪᒍ ᐊᒥᕆᐃ ᐱᐊᖁᐸᕆ
ᓂᖅ. ᐃᓄᓂᑐ ᒪᐳᖅ ᑎᒍᐊᑕᐅᕐᒪᕐᖃᐅ, ᐊᑕᐅᕆ ᐱᑕ ᐱᖁᑕᒍ
ᐊᒪᒍ ᐊᓇᐸᑕ ᑎᒍᐊᖁᒍᓲᓂ ᐊᒪ ᒪᖃᐊᓂᓇ ᐊᒪᒍ ᑕᖃᐊ
ᑕᒪᒡᕐᖅ ᑐᖁᒍᒪᒍᕐᖃᐳᖅ. ᕐᒪᐊᐳᑕ ᑲᓇᒪ ᑐᖁᖃᐳᑐ ᐱᐊᖁᒪ.
ᐱᐊᖁᖅ ᐊᒪᖁ ᒪᓇ ᓇᐅᕆᓇᐃ, ᖃᖃ, ᖁᒪᖢᐊᑐᖅ, ᖃᒍᐊᑦ,

Kiawat, Ottochie and Nawpachee. Among those who are living I have only one daughter, Nawpachee. Except for Kaka who lives in camp in the old way, they all live here in Cape Dorset, and now I live with Kumwartok and his wife.

On Akudluk Island, where Namoonie was born, there was good hunting. There were no caribou but there were polar bear, walrus and seal. But I did not care for Akudluk – my relatives were all around Cape Dorset, and it was too hard to get the white man's food from the Bay. We had no tea, only meat. After a year we went back to Cape Dorset for a short time, and then to Ikirasaq where we were in camp with Peter Pitseolak and lots of families. I don't remember them all or how many there were; in those days we didn't bother counting people.

But my husband used to be a very busy man with the hunting and he didn't like to live with other people. There are many days in the year and we moved many times – maybe ten times a year. We would often camp at Natsilik,

ᐅᑐᑭ, ᐊ<ᕐᐊᓗ. ᑕᑯᓂ ᐃᓄᕐᓂ ᐊᑕᐅᓯᒥ ᑭᕐᐊᓂ
<ᓂᑲᑐᒪ, ᐊ<ᕐᒥ. ᑲᑲ ᑭᕐᐊᓂ ᐃᑲᓄᑕᑲᓯᑐᓯ ᐅᕿᕐᐊᐳ
ᑎᑎᒃ ᐃᓄᕐ.ᐃᓄᐊᑎ ᑕᒪ ᑭᒥᑕᐅᔭᕐ ᐊᒪᓗ ᒪᓇ ᒍᒍᐊᐳ
ᒍᓂᒥᐅᔭᕐᒪ ᓄᑕᓗᓂ ᐊᓇᖅᕐᒪ.

ᐊᒍᓗᒥ, ᑕᐃᑲᓂ ᓇᒍᐃᓇ ᐃᓄᑕᑕᐅᕐᖕᕐ ᑕᐃᑲᓂ ᐅᒪᕐᑲᕐᐊ
ᓚᐅᐳ. ᔪᔪᑲᖕᓗᓂ ᐃᓯ ᓇᓄᑲ<ᓚᐳ, ᐊᐊᐊᓂ ᓇᕐᓄᓗ.
ᐃᓯ ᐊᒍᓄᑲ ᐱᐅᕿᓯᐅᕐᕿᑕ -- ᐃᓯᑲ ᐃᓄᐊᑎ ᑭᓗᓂᓴᐅᕐᑕ
ᐊᒪᓗ ᐊᕿᐊᕿᓂᓄ ᖃᓄᓇᒃ ᓂᕿᓂ ᐱᕿᖕᕿᑲ ᓂᐳᐊᐊᓂᑕᓄ.
ᑎᑲᓯᐳᕿᔪ ᑕᐃᑲᓂ ᓂᕿᒥ ᑭᕐᐊᓂ. ᐊᖕᒍ ᐊᑕᐳᕐ ᐊᓂᒍᓚ
ᐳᑎᓚᐅᕿᔪ ᑭᓗ ᕿᑕ ᑕᐃᑲᓂᕐᑕ, ᐊᒪᓗ ᑕᒪᓚ ᐊᕿᓴᕿᔪ
ᓄᓚᐅᐳᔪᕿ ᑕᐃᑲᓂ ᔪᐱᒪᖕᑲᖕᑕᓇᖕᑕᓄ ᐱᓯ ᐱᕐᐳᓂᒥ ᐊᒪᓗ
ᐊᕐᕐᑕᓂ ᐃᓯᓂᒥ. ᐊᐳᓇᕐᑕᖕ ᐃᓄᐊᑎ ᐊᒪᓯᓄ ᖃᕐᐳᖕᕐᐊ
ᒪᒪᑕ ᐊᐳᑕᕐᑐᒪ, ᑕᐊᕿᒪᓂ ᑭᑎᕐᕐᐊᖕᕐ ᖃᒪᕐᕐᓂᕿᓄᑕᕐ.

ᑭᕐᐊᓂ ᐅᕙᒪ ᐊᖕᕐᐊᓗ ᓄᑭᑕᕐᐊᔪᕿᑲᐅᕿᔭᓕᕐ ᐊᔪᓇᕐᐊᕿᓂ
ᑕᐊᓚ ᐱᐳᖕᕿᑲᐅᕿᔪ ᓄᓇᑲᓂᑭᕿᐊᖕᕐ ᐊᕿᖕᓂᓄ ᐃᓄᓂ. ᐅᖕᒍᐃ
ᐊᕿᕿᕿᑲᐅᕿᕿᑲ ᐊᖕᒍᒥ ᐊᒪᓗ ᓄᕐᕿᑕᓄ ᐊᕿᕿᓯᑕ -- ᐃᒪᖕ
ᑎᐅ ᔪᕿᓄᐱᓄᑕ ᐊᖕᒍᒥ ᓄᖕᓚᕐᕿᑕᓄ. ᔪᐱᓯᓴᑲᓄ ᓇᕿᑕᒥ,

Woman and dogs.
Engraving, 1967

ᐊᒃᓇᒃ ᑭᒥᓗ
ᐅᑯᓯᓴᔭᒥ ᓴᓇᒍᐊᒐ, 1967

a place about a week's journey from Cape Dorset, near many lakes. It had the most beautiful drinking water, the most beautiful water I have ever found. We often went to Natsilik to hunt fish; and at Natsilik, too, there were many geese. Later on, white people we met from the Department of Transport used to go there, too, and some of them called it 'Ashoona's Land'. Today, sometimes Namoonie still goes to Natsilik – but now he flies by plane.

ᑕᐃᑯᒐ ᐱᓇᓯᐊᒍᓯᓚᒪᒥ ᐃᒋᕋᒋᐊᓚ ᑭᒐᓂ ᐱᓯᓂ ᑕᓯ ᐊᒥᓯ ᓴᓂᐊᓂ. ᑕᐃᑲᓂ ᐱᐅᓂᐸᒥ ᐃᒥᕋᓴᑕᑲᑐ ᐃᒥᒥᒃ. ᐱᐆᓂᐸᒃ ᐃᒥᒃ ᑕᑯᓚᐅᓯᒪᔭᓚᒪᕋᓂ ᐃᒥᓯᐊᑲᓂᐸ. ᓇᓯᓚᒧᐸᓚᐅᑐᒍ ᐃᑲᓗᓂᐊᑎᐊᓯᑕ, ᐊᒪᓗᑕᐅ ᑕᐃᑲᓂ ᓇᑦᓯᓚᒥ ᐊᒥᓱᓂᒃ ᓂᓚᑲᐸᓚᐅᒥᔦ. ᓯᐊᕈᓚᑎᓗᒍ ᑲᓗᓇᓗ ᑲᑎᓚᓚᐅᓯᒪᔪᒍ ᑕᑯᐊ ᓇᓚᑎᑯᓂ ᐃᑲᓇᐃᔭᑐ ᑕᐃᑯᒐᑲᑕᓚᐅᓯᒪᔦᑕᐅ ᐊᒪᓗ ᐃᓚᒋᓄ ᑕᐃᔭᐅᕙᓚᐅᑐᒃ ᐊᒃᓯᓇᑉ ᓄᓇᒐ. ᒪᓇ ᐃᓚᓂᑯᑦ ᓇᐅᒥᓇᐃ ᓯᓚ ᓇᓯᓚᒧᑲᑕᐅᒃ ᐃᓚ ᒪᓇᓚ ᑲᒐᑕᓯᑯᑦ ᑎᒥᑲᑕᓚᑐᒃ.

Sometimes we went to the islands near Cape Dorset for seal and walrus. Spring and autumn are the best times for this kind of hunting.

ᐃᓚᓂᑯᑦ ᑭᒐᐃᑦ ᓴᓂᐊᓂ ᓄᓇᑲᐸᓚᐅᑐᒍᑦ ᓇᓯᓯᐅᑎᐊᓯᑕ, ᐊᐃᕕᓯᐅᑎᐊᓯᒪᓯᑕᓗ. ᐅᐱᒐᓴᒥ ᐅᑭᐊᒃᓴᒥᓗ ᐱᐅᓂᐸᒍᕙᓗᓂ ᑕᒪᑐᒧᒐ ᐊᔨᒋᒋᑐᓂᒃ ᐊᒍᓇᓯᐊᓗᓂ.

Both in summer and winter we used to move a lot. In summer there were always very big mosquitoes. I have made many drawings of moving camp in summertime and I always put in the mosquitoes. I do not like insects.

ᑕᒪᐃᓂ ᐊᐅᔭᑯᑦ ᐅᑭᐊᑯᓗ ᐊᐅᓚᒋᓇᐸᓚᐅᑐᒍᑦ ᐊᒥᓯᕕᓯᑕ. ᐊᐅᔭᑯ ᑕᐃᒪᒪᒐ ᐊᒋᔦᐸᓗᓂ ᑭᑐᑎᐊᑲᐸᓚᐅᑐ. ᑎᑎᑐᔭᓯᒪᔦᒐ ᐊᐅᓚᑐᓂᒃ ᓄᓇᒧᑦ ᐊᐅᔭᐅᑎᓗᒍ ᐊᒪᓗ ᑕᐃᒪᒪᒐ ᐃᓚᓯᕙᓯᒐ ᑭᑐᑎᐊᓂᒃ. ᐱᐅᓴᔭᒋᑐᒐ ᑯᐱᕈᓂᒃ.

Sometimes, when we camped in a place for the first time, we would put up an 'inukshuk'. My father and Ashoona

ᐃᓚᓂᑯ ᑐᐱᓯᒪᓯᑕ ᑐᐱᓯᒪᕕᑎᓂ ᓯᕗᓚᒥ, ᐃᓚᕗᑲᑕᓚᐅᓯᒪᔦᒍᑦ ᐃᓄᒃᓯᓂ. ᐊᑕᑕᒐ ᐊᒃᓯᓇᓗ ᑕᒪᒥ ᐊᑭᓯᐃᕙᓚᐅᑐᒃ

both built them from time to time, and Kumwartok built one a few weeks ago when he camped for the first time at a new place near Akudluk Island. A few years ago people from the Co-op built inukshuks above Cape Dorset, and these reminded me of the ones we used to make and I drew some for the prints.

In the old days we had different kinds of housing for the different seasons. We had the igloo, the 'kaamuk', which is a tent-hut, and the summer tents.

In winter I didn't mind whether we had an igloo or a kaamuk so long as we had a shelter for our family.

To build an igloo you have to have the right snow, but what kind of snow I don't know. Men built the igloos. I remember when I was a little girl I once built an igloo myself, but it was a funny-looking igloo – skinny and tall! Perhaps they take an hour to build, but in those days we didn't have watches. It is better to know the time. It used to be okay

ᑐᐱᖃᐊᕐᖓᓂ ᐊᓂᕒᒐᐅᐸᖄᐊᑐᐅ ᐊᒪᓗ ᑰᒪᑐ ᐊᓂᕒᒐᐅᑐᕒᐊ
ᐱᓇᕐᐊᑐᕐᐊᑯ ᐊᒥᕐᑎᐅ ᓇᐱᓕᓐᒪᓂ ᑐᐱᕒᒪᕐᕒᐊᒪᑕᓂ
ᓇᒥ ᓄᐊᒥ ᐊᑯᑕ ᓴᓇᐊᐱᓂ. ᐊᕒᒐᐊ ᐊᒥᕐᑎ ᐊᓇᒧᕒ
ᒪᑕᓂ ᐊᐅᐊ ᑰᐅᐊᖅᒪᐅ ᐊᓄᖃᕒᓴᐅᐅᕒᒪᕒ ᑭᒪ
ᓇᓴ ᐊᒪᓗ ᑕᖃ ᐊᖃᐊᒧᑎᕒᓴᐅᓯᑭ ᐊᓄᖃᕒᓴᐊᕐᓴᐊᐅᑎᓂ
ᑕᒪᒪ ᐊᓯᕒᓂᖅ ᑎᑎᑐᑕᐅᑐᒪ ᐊᓗᓂ ᐊᐸᓴᐅᒪ.

ᐅᖃᕒᐊᑎᓇᒧ ᐊᖃᕒᕒᐊᓂ ᐊᖅ ᖃᖅᐸᓴᐅᑐᒧ ᐅᑭᐅᒪ ᐅᐊᒪᒃᒪ
ᐊᐅᖅᒪᒧ. ᐊᐅᑎᒥ ᐊᖅ ᓴᐅᒪᖅᓴᑕ, ᑲᒪᕐ ᑐᐱᐅᓇᒥ ᓄᒥ,
ᐊᒪᓗ ᐊᐅᖅᒧᕒ ᑐᐱᕒᐅᒧᕒᓴᑕ.

ᐅᑭᐅᒧ ᖃᓴᐅᖅᐸᓴᐅᑐᒪᐅ ᕒᖅᕐ ᐊᐅᕐ ᐊᖅ ᓴᐅᒪᖅᐸᓴᐅᕐᑕ
ᐅᖅᓂ ᑲᒪᕐᖃᒧ ᖃᑕᓴᖃ ᐅᖃᒧᑎᖃᐸᓴᐅᕐᕐᑕ ᑭᐅᕒᓂᒥ.

ᐊᐅᑎᒥ ᐊᖅ ᓴᐅᒪᒪᑕᓴᒪ ᓇᒧᕒ ᐊᐅᕒᖕ ᐊᐅᑎᐊᒧᖅ ᐊᓂ
ᖃᓇᐅᒧᒪᒪ ᐊᐅᑎ ᖃᖅᐸᒥᑐᒪ. ᐊᒧᑎ ᐊᖅ ᓴᐅᒪᖃᕒᒪᑕᑎ.
ᐊᐅᓴᕐᐊᒧ ᓂᐊᖃᕒᐊᒧᕒᒪ ᐊᖃᓴᐅᒪᖃᐅᕒᒪᒪᒧ ᐊᑕᐅᕒᐊᒪ
ᑭᕒᐊᒧᓂ ᐊᖅ ᓴᐅᒪᓂᒧᕒᕐᖃᐅᕒᒪᒧᕒ -- ᐊᕒᑐᕒᐊᒧᓂ
ᑕᖅᕒᖃᐅᕒᒪᕐᕒ! ᐊᒪᖃ ᐊᖅᐸᓂᒪᕒᒥ ᐊᖅ ᓴᐅᒪᖃᕒᒧᕒᕒᕐᖅᐅᕐᑕ
ᐊᒪ ᑕᖃᒪᓂᐅᑎᓂᒧ ᐅᕐᕒᖃᕒᐸᓂᖃᑕ ᑕᒥᕒᖃᐅᕒᕒᖃ.ᐱᐅᓂᕒᐅ

It was good to have a new snow house.   ᐄᓄᒪᒃᑎᕆᒡᔪᐊᕐᒃ ᐱᐅᓯᓕᐳᑐᒃ
Felt pen, 1970   ᐊᑊᓯᒍ ᐊᔨᐳᐱᒍ ᑎᑎᑐᒪ, I970

Around the igloo.   ᐃᒃ ᓄᐱᒪᐸᑦ ᓯᓪᑕ
Engraving, 1964   ᐅᑯᕐᑦᕐᒥ ᑎᑎᑐᒪ, I964

without clocks, but it is okay with clocks, too. Now I am used to watching the time. The igloo would last all winter but often it would melt and drip inside from the heat of the kudlik. We used to dig a trench around the base to catch the water, and the women would scrape the soft snow from the walls inside with their 'ulus', the women's knives.

It was good to have a new snow house built because they were easy to clean – and very clean. But sometimes, if it was windy, the wind blew holes in the snow house, so perhaps the kaamuk was more comfortable.

To make the kaamuk, we would put up a tent and line the inside with wood. Between the tent and the wood we would put little bushes – sometimes blueberry bushes – to make it warm. I remember when Kumwartok, my son, got married. He and his wife were building the hut and she was carrying the bushes on her back. They were too heavy for her and she fell down, covered in bushes. They laughed. They were happy, building the hut together.

ᑎᓄᒍ ᑲᕐᒍᒪᒪ ᑲᐅᖅᒪᒥᕐᐊᕐ. ᑲᓄᐊᖳᐊᐳᕐᒥᕐᔪ ᒃᕐᒍᖳᖳᑲᑕ ᐃᓚ ᑲᓄᐊᒥᕐᒉᖅ ᒃᕐᒍᖳᖳᒃᔪᓂ. ᒪᓚᖳ ᕐᕐᐅᕐᕐᒪᐳᖩ ᒃᑲᕐᓯᒪᕐᐊᕐ ᑲᕐᒍᒪᒪ. ᐃᖅ ᓄᐊᒪ ᐅᖀᐳᒉᒪ ᐊᒡᒍᖧᐊᕐᐳᕐ ᐃᒉᓂ ᕐᕐᐊᓂ ᐃᖅ ᓄᐊᒪ ᐊᐳᕐᕐᐅᕐ ᒃᕐᕐᓄᓂ ᐃᓄᐊᒍ ᒃᐅᐳᕐ ᐅᖩᓂᓂ. ᐳᐊᑎᕐᕐᖩᐳᒍ ᐃᓄᐊᒪ ᑲᑕᒥᒃᕐᐊᕐᒉ ᐃᒥᑎᑕᐊᖧᕐᔪ ᐊᖩᓂ ᐊᕐᓴᓂ ᐃᔭᐊᕐᖅᐳᒍ ᐊᐳᑎᕐᐊᑎ ᐊᕐᒍᒥ ᐊᕐᓚᒥ ᐃᖅ ᓄᐊᐳᕐ ᐃᓴᖧᓂ ᐅᓂᓂ. ᐊᐳᖧᐅᕐᕐ ᓄᐸᒥ ᐃᖅ ᓄᐊᒪᒃᑲᕐᒥᐳᕐᐊᕐ ᕐᓴᓕᕐᒍᒪ ᐊᖩᐳᖧᐅᐳᕐᒪᐸᒉ, ᐊᒪᓚ ᕐᓴᓂᒉᐊᓯᕐᑎᓂᖅ. ᐃᖤᖩᕐ ᕐᕐᐊᓂ ᐊᖩᖳᒪᒪᖧ ᕐᐳᐸᑎ ᐳᐊᒥ ᐃᐳᕐ ᐃᖅ ᓄᐊᓕᒥ ᑕᐊᒪ ᐃᓚᒃ ᒉᓂ ᒃᐳᒍ ᐊᕐᐊᓄᕐᐳᖧᐊᖧᓂᒃ.

ᒃᐳᒉᐳᕐᒉ ᐳᐱᕐᐳᖧᒉᐳᐳᒍ, ᐊᒪᓚ ᐳᑭᓚᐊᐳᓂᒃ ᐃᓄᐊᒍᖍ ᕐᔅᕐᕐᒍ. ᐊᒡᓂᒉᒍᖍ ᐳᐱᐳᖧ ᕐᔅᓄ ᓄᐊᖳᑉᐊᕐᕐᒍ -- ᐃᒉᓂ ᕐᐳᑲᒡᐊᓂ ᓄᐊᖳᕐᕐᒍ ᐳᑯᕐᓂᐊᖩᖤ. ᐊᕐᒉᕐᕐᐊᖩ ᕐᐊᕐᖳᓂ ᐃᖅᓂᒪ ᒍᖳᐊᕐ, ᓄᕐᐊᒃᓚᒥ ᓄᕐᐊᖳᓂ ᐃᖅ ᓄᒉᐳᒉ ᐅᕐᒉᐊᕐ ᒃᒍᒥ ᑕᐊᒪ ᓄᕐᐊᖳᒥ ᓄᓚᒉᐳᕐᒉ ᓄᐊᖳᓂ. ᓄᐊᖳᓂ ᓄᓚᕐᕐᒥᓂ ᐅᒍᓚᐃᕐᓄᐊᓕᕐ ᓄᓚᕐᕐᒥᓂᖍ ᐸᑎᑎᐳᒉᐳᕐᖳᒉ ᓚᐳᖍ ᓂ ᓄᐊᖳᓂᒃ. ᐃᒉᐳᕐᖳᒉᒉ ᐊᕐᒉᐳᕐᖳᒉᒉ. ᒍᐊᒡᕐᒉᐳᕐᐳ, ᐃᖅ ᓄᐳᐳᑎ ᒃᒍᒥ ᑲᐳᕐᕐᑎᓂᒃ.

In the kaamuk we put a window. We made the window
from the intestine of the whale. We would clean it and blow
it up with air and hang it up to dry in long pieces. This
made a good window. It was also from the whale intestine
that we made sails for the sealskin boats.

In the summers before I was married I lived in a great
big sealskin tent made from the 'udjuk', the square-flipper
seal. These tents were so large they used to be used by
two families. Inside there was a great room and usually
the children slept on the 'kilu', the sleeping platform, at
the back of the tent and far away from the door. The
grown-ups slept just in front of the kilu on the 'ilukatigit',
which means 'both sides of the tent'. This was a sleeping
platform for two families or four grown-ups.

The sealskin tent was changed every summer because
it would dry out and then it was very hard to use. I used to
see my mother make these tents. She would scrape
the udjuk three times with the ulu and sew the skins on

ᑲᔪᒥ ᐃᖅ ᓗᑕᐅᕐᑕ ᐃᓚᑦᑐᐅᕝᑕᑕᐅᑐᒍ. ᐃᓚᑦᑐᐅᕐᑕ ᐊᑐᕝᑕ
ᐅᑐᒍ ᑭᓴᓗᐅ ᐊᑭᐊᒍᒪᓂ.ᓴᓗᒪᕝᕐᒍ ᐊᒪᓴ ᑎᑐᕝᒍ
ᕐᓴᒥ ᑲᓚᑲᓚᕐᒍ ᕑᓴᕐᐊᑎᕐᒍ ᑕᕐᕐᑎᐅᑎᓴᒍ. ᑲᓂ
ᐃᓚᕐᕐᐊᒍᕝᑕᐅᑐᖅ. ᐊᒪᓴᑐᖅ ᑭᓴᓗᐅᕐ ᐊᑭᐊᑊᓗᖅ
(ᐃᖅᕐᓕᓂ) ᑎᕐᕐᐅᑕᑐᐅᕝᑕᑕᐅᑐᒍ ᑭᕐᓗ ᐅᕐᐊᖅᓄ ᑎᕐᕐᐅᑕ
ᒍᐊᑎᕐᕑᕐ.

ᐊᐅᔭᒃ ᐅᐱᑕᑐᑎᖅᓗ ᐊᓄᕐᑊᑕᐅᕑᓚᕝᒍ ᐊᕐᕝᐊᒍᕐ ᑭᕐᕐ
ᐅᕝ ᑭᓕᓂ. ᑕᑦᐊ ᑐᐊᐢ ᐊᕐᕝᕐᓗᕝᑕᐅᑐ ᐊᑐᑕᐅᕐᑕᐅᑐ
ᒪᐅᐅᑐᕐ ᑭᑐᓚᓄ. ᐊᓗᑦᖅ ᐊᕐᕝᐊᒍᕐᕐ ᐃᓄᕐᓴᓇ ᐊᒪᓴ
ᐱᕝᓴᐊ ᑭᓴᑦᖅ ᕐᓇᕐᓗᑎ ᑭᓴᕐᐅᕐᑕᐅᕝᑕᐅᑐ. ᐃᓇᐃ ᐃᖅᓕᑎ
ᕐᓇᕐᑕᐅᑐ ᑭᑐᕐ ᕐᓗᓂ ᑭᕐᓴᖅ. ᐃᖅ ᓗᑲᑎᕐᑎ ᕐᐅᑲᑎᕐᐱ
ᐅᕐᑕᐅᑐ ᒪᐅᐅᓇ ᑭᑐᓚᓄ ᐅᕐᓗᓄ ᕐᑲᓗᓄ ᐃᐅᓚᓄᓄ.

ᐊᕐᕐᐅᕝ ᑭᕐᓚ ᑐᐊᖅ ᐊᕐᖅᕐᕐᐊᖅᕝᑕᐅᑐ ᐊᐅᕝᑲᓚᕑ ᕑᐊᓗᐊᓄ
ᐊᕐᓚ ᐊᒪᓴ ᐊᖅᐅᕐᑐᓚᕐᐊᕐᓗᒍ ᐊᑐᕐᐊᓗ. ᑕᑦᐊᕝᑕᐅᑐᒪ
ᐊᓄᓄᖅ ᑕᐊᒪᐊᑐᕐ ᑐᐱᑕᐅᑐᕐ. ᐅᖅ ᕐᐅᖅᕝᐅᕐᓂ ᕐᑲᕐᓄᓇ

Talilayu who keeps the sea animals
away from the hunters.
Felt pen, ca. 1967

ᑕᓕᓚᔦᒃ ᐃᒪᐅᑉ ᐅᒪᔦᒥᓂᒃ ᐅᒪᔦᓂᐊ
ᑎᓄᑦ ᐱᔭᐅᒍᓇᑎᓯᒋᑐ ᐃᒪᓂᒧ ᐊᓚᐅᑎ
ᒧᑦ ᑎᑎᑐᒐ, 1967 ᐅᑎᓗᒍ

We used to hang up the intestine
of the whale in long strips to dry.
Felt pen, ca. 1967

ᑭᓚᓗᒐᐃᑦ ᐃᓇᓗᐊᒥᓂᒃ ᐸᓂᓯᕙᓚᐅᑐᒍ
ᐃᒪᓂᒧ ᐊᓚᐅᑎᒧ ᑎᑎᑐᒐ,
1967 ᐅᑎᓗᒍ

the ground. These skins could dry out very quickly, too, so damp moss would be brought from the tundra to cover them as she worked.

The first year I was married I made a sealskin tent just for our family. I made only this one because, at the time, my mother used to stay in turns in our camp and in the camps of her sons. She would help me with all the sewing. Every year she made us a tent. Then, when I had four children, they began to sell canvas at the Bay. Ashoona was always able to buy canvas and so, after this, I made canvas tents. The last tents I made were for Jim Houston when he was here. One summer a group of white people – I think they were the first tourists – came and spent all summer camping here outside Cape Dorset. Eskimo families went and lived with them. I made about six tents.

In the old way, of course, women also made the boats. I never sewed for a sealskin boat but I used to sew for the

ᐅᕝᑭᒥ ᐱᓕᕆᐊᕆᓂ ᐅᒍᕐᓄᑦ ᒥᕐᑲᓕᕆᒍᓗ ᑭᕆ.ᑕᑦᐊ ᑭᕐᑦ
ᐸᓄᓴᐅᑎᑦᐊᐱᒍᓂᕐᓄᑦᐊᐅᑐᐅᕐ ᑕᐅᓪ ᑲᐅᕐᒍᑖ ᓄᐊᕝᑐᕐ ᐊᑭᓐᑎ
ᕐᐊᕐᐅᑐ ᓄᐊᕝᕐᒥᑦ ᑎᒥᒥ ᒧᒍᒍ ᑕᐅᓚ ᐱᐊᕆᕐᐊᑐᑦᐊᐱ.

ᕐᐅᓪᐊᕈ ᐊᕉᑎᒥ ᐅᐊᓄᑦᕐᑐᕆᓘ ᐊᕐᓴᕐ ᑭᕐᒥ ᑐᐊᓐᐅᑐᐅᕐ
ᓛᓪ ᑭᑐᓪᕐᓄᑦ ᑭᕐᐊᓄ ᑐᐊᓐᑎᓂ. ᑕᓄ ᓴᓀᑐᕐᓚᕐ
ᑭᕐᐊᓄ ᑕᐅᕐᓘᓂᐅᑎᓄᒍ ᐊᓘᓘ ᑐᐊᓐᓂᑦᑕᑦᐅᕐᓚᒪ ᐊᒡᓘ
ᐊᑦᓀᑦᑕ ᑐᐊᕈᓄᕐᐊᕐᓀ.ᐊᑦᕐᑦᑕᑕᑦᐅᕐᓚᕐᓘ ᐱᓇᕐᓚᓴᓘ.
ᐊᕈᒍᑕᓪᑕ ᑐᐊᓂᐅᑦᑦᑕᑦᐅᕐᓚᕐ ᐅᕐᓯᓂ. ᑕᐅᓪ ᑕᐊᕐᓚᓂ
ᕐᓚᓘᑦ ᐱᐊᕐᓴᑕᓂᓘᓪ, ᑐᐊᕐᓴᓴᕐ ᓄᐅᐊᕐᓴᑦᑐᕐᓚᕐᑦ
ᓄᐅᐊᐊᕐ. ᐊᕐᕐᓘᕐ ᑕᐊᓪᓪ ᓄᐅᐊᑐᓄᕐᑕᑐᑦ ᐊᓘ ᑕᐅᓪ
ᑐᐊᕐᓴᑕᑐᐊᕈ ᑐᐊᓐᑐᐊᕐᓄᑕᑐᑦᓘ. ᑭᓘᒥ ᑐᐊᓐᑕᓘ ᓴᓂᑐᐅᕐ
ᕐᓚᕐᓘ ᓴᐅᕐᒍ ᕐᐊᕐᐱ ᕐᐱᑕᓂ – ᓘ ᑕᓘᓂᑐᒍ. ᐊᐅᕐᑐᑦ
ᑭᓄᓂᑦ ᐱᑭᓀᑐᑎ ᓐᑭᓚᐅᕐᓚᕐᐊ ᑕᓘᐅᓪ ᕐᐅᓪᐊᐅᓂᑐᐅᕐᓚᕐᑐᑦ
ᓄᐅᕐᕐᓘᕐᓂᑦ – ᓐᑭᓂᒥ ᑕᓘᓚᓘᕐᓚᕐᐊ ᐊᐅᕐᓴᓘᓪ ᐅᐊᐅᕐᓘᓂ
ᑕᓘᓂ ᑭᓘᐊᑦ ᕐᑐᑕᓂ. ᐊᓪᓄᑦ ᑭᑐᓂᓂᐅ ᐊᐅᐊᐅᑐᐅᕐᓚᕐᑦ
ᑐᐊᕐᓚᑭᓐᑎᕐᓚᕐᐊᑐᕐᓂ. ᑐᐊᓐᐅᑐᐅᕐᓚᕐᓘ ᐱᓕᕐᐊᑐᕐᓴᓄᕐ.

ᐅᐊᕐᐊᑐᑐᑦ, ᕐᑭᐅᓘ, ᐊᕐᐊᐅᑕᑐ ᒥᕐᕐᑦᕐᓚᕐ.
ᒥᕐᑐᐅᕐᓚᕐᓴᑐᓗᑕᐊᕐᐅᑦ ᑭᕐᓘᕐ ᐅᒥᐊᓪ ᑭᕐᒪ ᑭᕐᐊᓄ

We would sew covers for kayaks with sinew from the caribou leg muscle. Coloured pencil and felt pen, ca. 1967

ᖃᔭᑕᐅᖅᑕ ᑐᑐᑦ ᓂᕐᒧᖕ ᐃᕕᒃᑲ
ᓇᑎᖅᔪᑦ ᑕᖅᓴᓂᐊ ᐊᓇᐅᑎᓄᑦ ᐊᒪ
ᐃᒪᓪᒧ ᑎᑎᖅᒪ, 1967 ᐅᑐᖒ

kayaks. In the old days, usually the women would row the sealskin boat and the men would go in the kayaks. In one drawing, I have shown the women's boat towing a kayak. If it became rough they would take the kayak-man aboard. In this print, all around the boats are little pests. What are they doing there? It is their business to be there. Did Eskimos believe in spirits and pests and monsters? Maybe they did. In the old days there was much to fear.

In the old days I was never done with the sewing. There were the tents and the kayaks, and there were all the clothes which were made from the different skins – seal, caribou and walrus. From skins we also made cups for drinking and buckets for carrying water. And when we caught geese we used to make brooms for cleaning from the wings which we bound together. If we had enough brooms we would throw the wings away.

As soon as I was finished sewing one thing, I was always sewing another. Sometimes, when I was very busy with

ᒥᕐᓴᑲᐅᑐᒐ. ᐅᕿᕐᐊᑎᓄᒍ ᐊᖃᓄᐊᑦ ᐸᑕᖃᐅᑐ ᓇᕐᐅᑦ ᑭᕐᓗᖅ ᐅᒥᐊᒥ ᐊᒪᓗ ᐊᔪᑎᑦ ᖃᔭᑐᓄᕐᑦ. ᐊᑕᐅᓯᒃ ᑎᑎᑐᖅᕐᒪᕐ ᐅᕐᓴᔪᕐᒪᕐ ᑎᑎᑐᕐᒥ ᓴᓇᕐᓚᖅᑐ ᑕᒃᓯᐅ ᑎᕐᕃ ᐊᖃᓄᐊᑦ ᐅᒥᐊᒪ ᐅᓂᐊᑐᖅ ᖃᔭᒥᖅ. ᐊᑯᓇᕐᑐᐊᒪᕐ ᐊᖃᓄᐊᑦ ᐃᑭᑎᕐᕿᑲᐅᑐᑦ ᖃᔭᑐᓄᖅ. ᑕᕐᒪ ᑎᑎᑐᕐᒥ, ᐃᓄᐊᒍ ᐅᒥᐊᕐᖅ ᒥᑭᑐᐊᕐᔪᓄ ᐅᒪᔪᖃᖅᓄ. ᓴᓇᕐᐊᑦ ᑕᐃᒃᓄ? ᐃᖃᓇᐃᖅᓂᒪᕐᐅᖅ ᑕᐃᒃᓄ. ᐃᓄᐊᑦ ᐅᐱᑎᖃᐸᕐᑦ ᐊᓪᑐᓂ ᐅᒪᕐᑐᓗ ᐃᓄᓴᓄ? ᐊᒪᒃ ᐅᐱᐊᑐᕐᓂ. ᐅᕐᓴᐊᑎ ᓄᔪ ᐊᕐᓇᐅᑕᖅᑲᐅᑐᒪᓪ. ᐅᕐᓴᐊᑎᓄᒍ ᒥᕐᓴᔪᖅᑲᐅᑐᒐ. ᑐᐱᖅᑲᐅᑐᒍ ᖃᖃᓄ ᐊᒪᓗ ᐃᓄᒪᕐ ᐊᓄᓴ ᓴᓄᕐᓚᖅᓄ ᐊᐱᕐᕐᑐᖕᖅ ᐱᕐᓄᐊᓄᓂ, ᑐᑐᓄ, ᐊᐃᐊᓂᓄ. ᐱᕐᐃᓇᖕᖅ ᓴᓇᕿᑎᕐᓄᐅᖅ ᐊᒥᑐᑎᑐᕐᐅᖕᖅ ᐊᒥᑎᐅᑎᑐᕐᖕᖅᓂ. ᐊᒪᓗ ᑲᐅᖅᑕᖅ ᓴᓄᐅᑎᓄᐅᖃᑲᐅᑎᕐᓄᐃᖅ ᐃᖕᓴᓄ ᑭᓇᑎᕐᖕ ᓴᓄᐅᑎᐅᖃᑲᐅᑐ. ᓴᓄᐅᑎᖕᓄ ᓇᓗᑐᑲᑐᐊᑐᕐᑦ ᐃᖕᓴᐃ ᐊᑎᕆᑲᐅᑐᕐᑦ.

ᐊᑕᐅᓯᒥ ᒥᕐᑎᓴᐊᒪᒪ, ᐊᕐᐊᓂ ᒥᕐᑎᐊᕐᕃᑲᐅᑐᒪ ᑕᐃᒪᒪ. ᐃᓇᓄᒍ ᐊᖃᕐᐊᓗ ᒥᕐᓴᐊᓂᒪᒪ ᐅᐊᓄᖕ ᐃᑲᕿᑕᐅᖃᑲᐅᑐᒪ. ᐊᑎᕆᑕᐅᑐᒍ ᐃᑲᕿᑲᐅᑕᒪ.

Happy girls.
Felt pen, ca. 1967

A bird from my mind.
Felt pen, 1968

ᓂᕕᐊᓯᐊᒃ ᑯᕕᐊᓯᑐᒃ
ᐃᒪᓂᒧ ᐊᓚᐅᑎᒧᑦ ᑎᑎᑐᒐ,
I967 ᐅᑎᓗᒍ

ᐃᓯᒪᒐᓂ ᑯᐸᓄᐊᒃ
ᐊᓚᐅᑎᒧ ᐃᒪᓂᒧ ᑎᑎᑐᒐ, I968

Three birds.
Felt pen, ca. 1967

ᗪ<ᓄᐊᶜ ᐱᑕᕐᶜ
ᐊᒪᶜᒎ ᐊᒡᐅᑎᒎ ᑎᑎᑐᒪ,
I967 ᐅᑎᒎ

the sewing, my husband would help me. He used to help me with the parkas.

This is how we used to make our clothing. The men would take the skins from the animals and the women would scrape them with the ulus. When I was a young girl and had just married, I did my first sealskin, which was a young, square-flipper seal. I was scraping this seal very quickly and, when it was finished and I stretched it for drying, I saw hundreds of holes! The skin had not been done properly. But I did not do that twice. I tried hard to learn how to sew because I envied the women who could sew nicely. We bought needles from the Bay but we made thread from the whale muscle which was soaked in sea-water and we also used strips of the caribou skin. The clothes could be made out of any kind of skin – caribou, seal or walrus – but I liked the lovely caribou best.

We also had duffel. I do not remember exactly when the duffel came, but I remember having a duffel parka as a

ᑕᐊᒪᓇᑕᒪ ᐊᓄᓕᓄ ᓇᓇᐸᒡᐅᑐᒎᶜ. ᐊᒎᑎᶜ ᐱᒉᐸᐅᑐᶜ
ᐅᒪᐊᓄᵇ ᐊᒥᒥᓄᵇ ᐱᕐᓇᑎᵇ ᐊᒪᒎ ᐊᑳᓇᐊᶜ ᑭᕐᑎᐸᶜᐅᑕᕐ
ᐅᵇ ᒎᒎ. ᑕᐊᕐᒪᓄ ᓄᐱᐊᕐᐊᒎᕐᒪ ᐅᐊᑕᑭᕐᐅᕐᒪᓗ ᕐᐳᖤ<ᕐᒥ
ᓇᕐᐅᶜ ᑭᕐᒪᓄ ᓇᕐᐊᒥᵇ ᑭᕐᑎᐸᐅᕐᒪᐊᒪ ᑕᕐᒥᒪ ᑭᕐᒪᵇ
ᐊᵇ ᕐᐊᒎ ᕐᑭᕐᒪ ᑕᐊᒪ ᐱᓇᓇᕐᑯ ᐊᓄᐸᐅᕐᒪᕐᒪ <ᓄᕐᐊᑎᕐ
ᕐᒎ, ᑕᑯᓇᐸᕐᒪᕐᒪ ᑭᑕᐸᓄᓄ ᐊᒥᕐᐊᓄᵇᵇ! ᑕᓇ ᑭᕐᵇ
ᐱᕐᐊᓄᕐᑕᓗ. ᐊᓇ ᑕᐊᒪᐊᓄᑭᕐᐅᕐᑎᐅᒪ ᑭᒎᕐᒥ. ᐊᓇᓄᐊᕐ
ᐊᓵᕐᐊᒎᓇᓇᕐᐅᕐᒪᕐᒪ ᐊᕐᒪᒪ ᐊᵇᓇᵇ ᒥᕐᕐᐊᒎᕐᑕᕐᵇ.
ᓄᐅᐱᕐᐊᕐᶜ ᒥᕐᐅᑎᓇᵇ ᓄᐅᐅᐊᒥ ᑭᕐᐊᓄᓇ ᐊᕐᒎᓄᐅᑕᐸᐅᑐᒎᶜ
ᑭᕐᓗᐅᐸᶜ ᓄᑭᕐᓄ ᑭᓄᕐᐊᑎᕐᒎ ᑕᑎᒎ ᐊᒪᒎ ᐊᒪᓄᑕᐅᵇ
ᐊᑐ<ᕐᐊᐅᕐᒥᕐᒎ ᑐᑐᶜ ᐊᕐᒎᕐᓄ. ᐊᓄᓵᕐᐅ<ᕐᐊᐅᑐᒎ ᑲᓇᐊᓇ
ᑭᕐᒪᵇ -- ᑐᑐᕐᓄ ᓇᕐᕐᓄ ᐊᑕᐊᐊᓄᕐᒪᓄ ᐊᓇ ᑐᑐᕐᵇ
ᐱᐅᕐᓄᕐᐊᐅᕐᒪᕐᒪ.

ᐊᓄᕐᕐᕐᵇᕆ<ᕐᐅᕐᐊᒎᑕᐅᵇ. ᐊᐅᕐᐊᕐᕐᑎᐅᒪ ᕐᒪ ᐊᓄᕐᕐᵇ
ᑎᕐᓄᒪᒪ, ᐊᓇ ᐊᐅᕐᐊᕐᒪ ᐊᓄᕐᑭᕐᒪ ᐊᓄᕐᕐᕐᒥᕆ ᓄᐱᐊᕐᒪ

little girl. Probably, when the Hudson's Bay post came here, the duffel came along with the company. The duffel was used for the inner parka and for the duffel socks.

Each person wore two parkas. Before the duffel came, the first parka, the one nearest the skin, had the fur touching the skin, while the outer parka had the caribou hair outside. When the duffel came, we used it inside. We didn't have money often – we bought the duffel with fox skins.

When I made a parka I used to try to make it the way I wanted it to look. I would try to make it look very good. It was not easy and I used to sew on a parka for many days. We always used the finest skin of the young caribou for the head of the parka and, on top, we would put little ears from the baby caribou. It looked very nice. I would also make patterns and designs with different-coloured skins.

Before we started living in one place, as we do now, we used to walk very long distances and the boots would wear

ᑯᔭᕐᓗ. ᐃᓚᖕ ᑎᑯᔓᖅᐅᖘᖑ ᖔᐅᐱᓐᖁ ᑎᕿᑎᖑᒥ ᑕᒪᐅᓗ,
ᐊᑎᕐᖀ ᑎᑭᖁᐅᑯᒃᐳᐊᖔ ᖔᐅᐱᓐᑭᖚ. ᐊᑎᕐᖀ ᐊᑎᕐᑕ
ᐃᖚᐊᖓᑎᖚ ᐊᑐᑕᐅᓕᐅᑐ ᐊᒪᖚ ᐊᓕᐸᑎᐊᕐᒍ.

ᐊᑕᐅᖮ ᐃᖁᖿ ᐊᑎᕐᖁᖿ ᒪᖿᖿ ᐊᑐᖔᓕᐅᑐᖿ. ᐊᑎᕐᖀ
ᑎᑭᖁᐅᓇᒍ, ᖘᖧᓕᖓ ᐊᑎᕐ, ᐅᐱᖓᒍ ᖃᖓᒃ ᒥᑯᖘᓓᒍ,
ᒥᑯ ᐅᐱᖓᒍ ᐊᑐᐊᖓᒍ, ᖘᖧᒪ ᐊᑎᕐᑕ ᑐᑐᖮᐅᖿ ᒥᑯ
ᖘᓕᖖᖁᖔᖒ. ᐊᑎᕐᖀ ᑎᖕᒪ ᐊᑐᖓᐅᐱᖔ ᐃᖚᐊᑎᕐᒍ.
ᖀᖏᐅᖕᖁᐅᖃᖔ ᖔᐅᐱᖿᖁᖒᒍ ᐊᑎᕐᖀᒪ ᑎᑎᖓᖖᐊᖐᖒᖁ.

ᐊᑎᕐᓕᖁᖐᐆᖳᖳ ᐊᑭᖘᐊᖚᕐᐊᖿᖁᖒᖐ ᖃᖔᐊᐄᖚᖕᖓ. ᐊᑭᖘᐊ
ᖚᕐᐊᖿᖁᖐᖐ ᐊᖃᖘᖐᖚ ᐱᐅᖧᖀᐊᑎᖚᖘᒍ. ᐱᐆ ᐃᖃᓐᐊᐱᖃᐅ
ᖘᒪᕐᖐᖿ ᐊᒪᖚ ᒥᖘᖁᐅᑐᖒᖐ ᐊᑎᕐᒥ ᐅᖃᖓᖖ ᐊᕐᖖᖔᖝ.
ᖃᐊᖐᖐᖿᖚ ᐊᐅᖘᐊᖁᐅᑐᒍᖢ ᐱᐅᖐᖕᖘᖐ ᑐᖐᐊᖐᕐ ᖃᖐᖘᐊᑎᕐᒍ
ᐊᑎᕐᒍᖐ ᐊᒪᖚ ᖃᖃᖕᔪᕐᒪ ᑐᖐᖘᐊᐅᖐ ᖘᐅᖔᑐᖒᖔᖖᖐ.
ᐱᐅᖘᖖᖚᖘᖁᖐ. ᐅᖃ ᑐᖖᖑᐅᖘᖔᖐᐅᖊᖡᖐ ᐊᑭᖘᒥᖒᖐᖒᖚ
ᐊᖃᖕᖁᖖ ᖃᖃᖃᖔᖒᖐ ᑐᖐᖘᐊᖐ.

ᐊᑕᐅᖘᖐᐄᖖᖄᖖᖐᖐᖖᖡᖤ ᖖᖕᖐ ᖃᐊᖔᖖᐃᖔᖡᖤ ᖚᖕᖐ ᐱᖐᖘᖁᖐᐆᖡ
ᐅᖚᖘᖐᖔᖚᒍ ᖃᖐᖗᖚᖚ ᖒᖡᖘᖐᖒᖐ ᐊᖐᖘᖐᖐ. ᐱᖐᖐᖐᖐᐅᖐᖐᖚᖘᖁᖐᖔᖐᖖ

On top of the parka we put little ears from the baby caribou.
Felt pen, 1970

ᑐᑐᔭᐱᐅᑉ ᓯᐅᑎᒋᓂ ᐊᑎᒋᐅᑉ ᓇᓴᒐᓄ ᓯᕙᓚᐅᑐᒍᑦ ᐃᒪᓕᒎᑦ ᐊᓚᐅᑎᒎᑦ
ᑎᑎᑐᒐ, 1970

Engraving, 1962

ᐅᑯᓯᓴᔭᒥ ᓴᓇᒍᐊᒐᒃ, 1962

out quickly. I was never finished with making mukluks. I also would make new soles and sew them on the worn boots. For boots we used only sealskin and, once the skin was cleaned, we would chew it so that the mukluks would be soft. It was hard to do but it worked well.

I also made 'qutugut', which were worn above the boots and covered the legs. This is how it used to be with qutugut – there was string with a knot on the end, which went up and hooked over the pants above.

When James Houston, whom we call Sowmik – the left-handed one – came to Cape Dorset and told me to draw the old ways, I began to put the old costumes into the drawings and prints. Some days I am really tired of the old ways – so much drawing. But many liked my parkas – many people really used to like my clothes.

I am too old now to make any more and my eyes are not good. But every year I still make sealskin pants for Kaka.

ᔪᒋᑐᒐ ᑲᒥᓕᐅᓯᒐ. ᓄᑕᓂᓗ ᐊᓚᐳᕙᓯᒐ ᑲᒥᑦ ᐊᓕᓯᒪᓂᒋᓂ ᒥᓯᐸᓯᒋ. ᑲᒥᑲᐸᓚᐅᑐᒍ ᓇᓯᒐᕕᓂᓂ ᑭᓯᐊᓂ ᑕᐃᒪ ᑭᓯᑦ ᓴᓗᒪᓴᑎᑐᐊᒐᑎᒍ ᑭᓂᑎᐸᓚᐅᑕᕗᑦ ᑲᒥᑦ ᑭᑐᑐᓂᐊᒪᑕ. ᐃᓯᐊᒋᑐᐊᓗᕙᓚᐅᔪᔪ ᐃᓚ ᐱᒍᓇᓯᐊᐸᓚᐅᔪᔪ.

ᑯᑐᒎᑦᓕᐅᐸᓚᐅᒥᔪᒐ ᑲᒥᑦ ᑯᓚᒐᓂᑎᓗᒍ ᐊᑐᑕᐅᕙᓚᐅᑐᒥᒃ ᓂᐅᒋᔭᑎᑯᑎᓂᒃ. ᑕᐃᒪᓇᑕᒐ ᑕᐃᒪᐃᑐᕙᓚᐅᓯᒪᔪᑦ ᑯᑐᒎᑦᓄ ᐊᒃᓯᓇᑲᓗᑎ ᑭᓚᓯᒪᓗᑎᒃ ᐃᓯᒥᒎᑦ, ᑕᐸᐅᒐᒐᔪᒥ ᑭᓚᓯᒪᓗᓂ ᑲᓕᑦ ᑯᓚᒐᒎᑦ.

ᑕᐃᓯᒪᓂ ᔭᐃᒥᓯ ᔪᓯᑕᓐ ᓴᐅᒥᐅᓂᖁᑕᐅᔪ, ᑭᒐᓄᒪ ᑕᐃᒪ ᐅᑲᐅᑎᓚᐅᓯᒪᔭᒐ ᑎᑎᑐᔭᑯᓯᓂᒐ ᐅᕙᓯᐊᕈᓂᑕᓂ ᐃᓕᓯᕙᓕᓚᐅᑐᒐ ᑎᑎᑐᔭᑐᓄᑦ ᐱᐅᓯᑐᑲᕕᓂᓂ ᑎᑎᑐᔭᓯᒪᔪᓄᓯᒋ ᐊᒪᓗ ᐊᐲᓕᐅᓯᒪᔪᓄ. ᐃᓚᓂ ᐊᒃᓯᐊᓗ ᑕᑲᓯᒪᕙᓗᒐ ᐅᕙᓯᐊᕈᓂᑕᓂ ᐊᒃᓯᐊᓗ ᑎᑎᑐᔭᑎᐊᓴ. ᐃᓚ ᐊᒥᓯᓄ ᐱᐅᒋᔭᐅᔪ ᐊᑎᒋᑲ ᐊᒥᓯᓄ ᐃᓄᓄᑦ ᐊᒃᓯᐊᓗ ᐱᐅᒋᔭᐅᕙᓚᐅᔪᔪ ᐊᓄᖁᑲ.

ᒪᓇᓕ ᓂᒋᐅᒍᒪ ᓴᓇᓚᐅᓯᒪᒍᓄᑐᒐ ᐃᐲᑲᓗ ᐱᐅᓯᐊᒍᓄᒪᑕ. ᐃᓚ ᓯᓕ ᐊᖁᒍᑕᒪ ᑲᓕᓕᐅᐸᑐᒐ ᓇᓯᔭᓂ ᑲᑲᐅᑉ ᑲᓕᓴᒋᓂ. ᐊᑕᑕᒥᑎᑐᑦ, ᑲᑲ ᓄᓇᑲᑎᑲᒎᒪᔭᒋᑐᑦ ᐃᓄᑲᑎᒥᓂᒃ ᐊᒪᓗ

Overleaf: ᒪᐱᑐᖄᐅ ᑐᒻᓕᑦᐊ

A bird for the doctor.   ᐊᓯ ᐊᒡᢞᐅᑎᒍᒡ ᒡᐸᓕᐊᑫ
Felt pen, 1971   ᐃᓕᒻᒍ ᐊᒡᐅᑎᒍᒡ ᑎᑎᒍᒪ, I97I

Thoughts of a bear.   ᐃᢞᓕᒡ ᓄᑲᐃᑉ
Felt pen, 1970   ᐃᓕᒻᒍ ᐊᒡᐅᑎᒍᒡ ᑎᑎᒍᒪ, I970

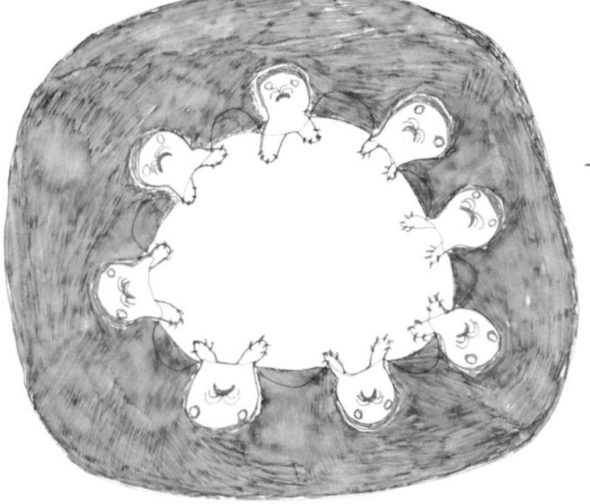

Bearded seals around ice.
Felt pen, ca. 1967

ᐅᔪᐃᑦ ᓯᑯᒥᑐᑦ
ᐃᒪᓕᒧ ᐊᓚᐅᑎᒧ ᑎᑎᑐᒐ,
1967 ᐅᑎᓗᒍ

Travelling by dog team (detail).
Coloured pencil and felt pen,
ca. 1967

ᑭᒧᓯᑐᑦ (ᐃᒪᐃᓕᒐᓂᒐ)
ᑕᒃᓴᓕᓄ ᐊᓚᐅᑎᓄ ᐊᒪᓗ ᐃᒪᓕᒧᑦ
ᑎᑎᑐᒐ, 1967 ᐅᑎᓗᒍ

Like his father, Kaka does not want to live with other people and he stays in camp. Like his father, Kaka is a very good hunter and every year he gets the most beautiful skins from a special seal – the 'kasigiak'. The skins are lovely and dark, and he brings them to me and I must make these pants.

I liked the old clothes but I like the new clothes, too.

In the old days men were very good hunters. They had to keep busy to feed the dogs and the family. We depended on the dogs and Ashoona always had a very good team. Dogs would have puppies and there were always from five to ten. They never had to be trained, they knew by instinct. They were clever and dangerous, too, but when they were full and happy, they went fast. Sometimes in the camps in a bad winter, the dogs used to starve, but Ashoona always brought lots of food. Some days he would bring ten seals from one day's hunting. He would cut meat for the dogs even in winter.

ᐃᒃ ᓗᑲᒋᑐᒥᑲᑕᑐᒃ. ᐊᑕᑕᒥᑎᑐ ᑲᑲ ᐊᒍᓇᓯᐊᓯᑎᐸᓗ ᐊᒪᓗ ᐊᕆᒍᑕᒪ ᐱᐅᔪᐸᓗᓂ ᓇᓯᐸᑐ ᒥᑯᓯᐊᑭᑐᐸᓗᓂ ᓇᓯᓂ -- ᑲᓯᒋᐊᓂ. ᑕᑯᐊ ᒥᑯᒋᑦ ᐱᐅᔪᐸᐃᓗᑦ ᑭᓂᓗᑎᓗ ᐊᒪᓗ ᑲᐃ ᓯᐸᓗᓂ ᑭᓯᓂᒃ ᑲᓕᓕᐊᓴᑲᓂᒃ.

ᐱᐅᓴᐸᓚᐅᑐᒐ ᐅᕙᓯᐊᕈᓂᑕᓂ ᐊᓄᕆᓂ, ᐃᓚ ᐱᐅᓴᒥᔪᒐᑕᐅᒃ ᓄᑕᓂ ᐊᓄᕆᓂ. ᐅᕙᓯᐊᕈ ᐊᒍᑎᑦ ᐊᒍᓇᓯᐊᓯᑎᐅᕙᓚᐅᔪᔪ. ᓄᑲᓚᐅᓯᒪᒋᓯᑎᒃ ᓂᒋᑲᐃᓯᑎᒃ ᑭᒥᓂ ᐃᓕᒥᓂᓗ. ᑭᒥᓂᒃ ᐃᑲᔪᑎᑲᓚᐅᑐ ᐊᒪᓗ ᐊᒃᓯᐊᓇ ᑌᒪᒐᓗ ᐱᐅᔪᓂ ᑭᒥᑲᐸᓗᓂ. ᑭᒥᑦ ᑭᒥᐊᕆᑕᐸᓗᑎ ᐊᒪᓗ ᑕᐃᒪᒐ ᑭᒥ 5-ᒍᓗᑎ 10-ᒍᓗ ᑎᓗᓂ. ᐃᓕᓴᒋᐊᑲᐸᓚᐅᒋᑐ, ᑲᐅᔨᒪᔪᐃ ᐊᐅᓚᓂᑐᐃᓇᒧ. ᐊᑭᑐᓯᓕᒐᒥ ᑯᕕᐊᓯᓕᒐᒥᓗ ᓯᑲᑐᕙᓚᐅᑐ. ᐃᓚᓂᑯ ᓄᓇᑎᓂ ᓯᓚ ᐱᐅᑎᓇᒍ ᑭᒥ ᑲᐸᓚᐅᑐ ᐃᓚ ᐊᒃᓯᓇ ᑕᐃᒪᒐ ᑎᑭᐅᔨᕙ ᓚᐅᑐ ᓂᑭᐊᓗᓂ -- ᐃᓚᓂ 10-ᓂ ᓇᓯᓂ ᐊᓇᕆᐅᔨᕙᓚᐅᑐᒃ ᐅᒃ ᓗᒥ ᐊᑕᐅᓯᒥ ᐊᒍᓇᓯᐊᓯᓂ. ᓇᓯᓂ ᐱᓚᐸᓚᐅᑐ ᑭᒥᓄᕆᓴ ᒥᓂᒃ ᐅᑭᐅᒐᓴᒥ.

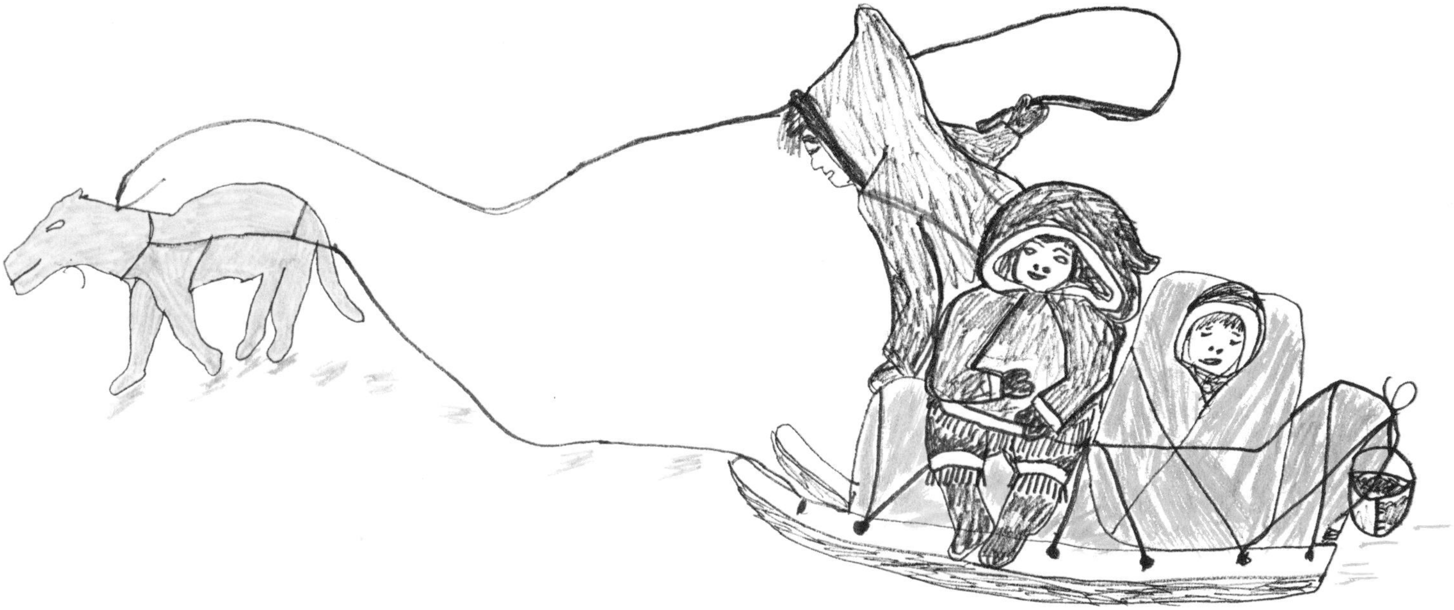

There seemed to be more animals in the old days. There were more whales and more seals and, just quite recently, there were lots of narwhales around Cape Dorset. But today the animals don't seem to come into the settlements much. Now they have all these motors and the animals hear them and run away. Now there are motors everywhere, but dogs were safer than skidoos. Skidoos can break down out there, far from Cape Dorset; and dogs will bark when they see a polar bear.

In the old days, when men left the camp, they would always give the women something that killed – a gun. But I used to be very poor at shooting and I remember one day, although we had lots of food, I wasted a whole box of ammunition trying to kill a little seal. I knew it would get away. But though I have never shot a caribou, there are very few birds that I have not caught.

When I was a little girl my father and mother taught me how to catch a goose. Four people would corner a goose

ᐅᕙᓯᐊᕈᑎᓗᒍ ᐅᒪᔪᑲᓂᓴᐅᔭᐸᓚᐅᑐᒃ. ᑭᓚᓗᒐᑲᓂ'ᐃᐅᓯᓂ ᐊᒪᓗ ᓇᓯᑲᓂᓴᐅᓯᓂ ᒪᓇᕋᑕ ᑭᓯᐊᓂ ᐊᒃ ᓗᑕᕋᑕᑲᒥ ᐊᒥᓯᓂ ᑭᒐᐃ ᓴᓂᐊᓂ. ᐃᓚ ᒪᓇ ᐅᒪᔪᐃ ᑎᑭᓯᐊᓚᐅᓯᒪᔪᔭᒍᓇᐃᑐ ᓄᓇᓕᓄ. ᒪᓇᓕ ᐊᒥᓯᓂ ᐊᐅᓚᐅᑎᑲᓕᒪᑕ ᐅᒪᔪᓄ ᑐᓴᔭᐅᑲᑕ ᒪᑕ ᑭᒪᓯᑲᑕᓯᑎᓗᒪᑕ. ᒪᓇᓕ ᐊᐅᓚᐅᑎᑲᓕᒪᑕ ᓇᒥᓕᒪᒃ, ᐃᓚ ᑭᒥ ᐊᑕᓇᐃᓂᓴᐃ ᓯᑭᑐᓂ. ᓯᑭᑐ ᑲᒧᑎᐅᔭᐃ ᓯᕋᒍᓇᑐ ᓇᒥᑐᐃᓇᒃ, ᑭᒐᐃᑦ ᐅᒐᓯᑕᓗᒐᓂ, ᐊᒪᓗ ᑭᒥᑦ ᒧᒍᕈᓇᑐ ᑕᑯᒐᐃᒐᒥ ᓇᓄᒥᒃ.

ᐅᕙᓯᐊᕈᑎᓗᒍ ᑕᐃᓯᒪᓂ ᐊᒍᑎᑦ ᑭᒪᐃᒐᒥ ᐊᓇᕋᒥᓂ ᑕᐃᒪᒐ ᐊᒃᓇᐃᑦ ᑐᑯᓯᒍᑎᓴᒐᓂ ᑐᓂᓯᕙᓚᐅᑐ -- ᑯᑭᐅᑎᒥ. ᐃᓚ ᓯᒋᐊᒍᓇᐸᓚᐅᒋᑐᒐ ᐊᒪᓗ ᐊᐅᓚᔭᔪᒐ ᐊᑕᐅᓯᐊᓯᒐ, ᓂᑭᓚᐊ ᓗᒐᓗᐊᓯᑕ, ᐊᓯᑭᓚᐅᓯᒪᔪᒐ ᐃᓗᐃᑐᒥᒃ ᐃᓯᕕᒥ ᓴᑯᑯᕕᒥ ᓇᓯᑯᓗᒥᒃ ᑐᑯᓯᒐᓯᐊᓯᒐ. ᑲᐅᔭᒪᓯᒐ ᓯᓚᒐᒋᒋᐊᒪ. ᐃᓚ ᓯᒋᐊᓚᓯᒪᒋᑲᓗᐊᑐᒐ ᑐᑐᒃᒥᒃ, ᐃᑭᑐᑯᓗᑲᑐᒃ ᑯᐸᓄᐊᓂᒃ ᑯᐸᓄᐊᓚᐅᒋᑕᓂᒃ ᐃᓄᓂᓚᒪᓂ.

ᑕᐃᓯᒪᓂ ᓂᕕᐊᓯᐊᑯᓗᑎᓗᒐ ᐊᑕᑕᓄ ᐊᓇᓇᓄᓗ ᐃᓕᓴᑕᐅᓚᐅᓯ ᒪᔪᒐ ᑲᓄ ᑎᒍᓯᓯᒍᒪᒐᑕ ᓂᓕᒥ. ᓯᑕᒪ ᐃᓄᐃ ᓯᓂᕈᒋᓯᑎ

My parents taught me how to catch a goose (Pitseolak, lower left; her father, top left; her mother, top right; and a woman from the camp).
Felt pen, 1970

ᐊᐋᓗᓂᑦ ᐊᑦᑕᒪᔾᓄ ᓂᑦᕐᐲᖅᐅᓂᑦᕐᐊᑦ ᐅᐳᒪ (ᐱᕐᐲᑕᓕ, ᐱᕐᐲᑕᒃ ᐊᑦᑕᒪ, ᐊᐋᒪᓕ, ᐊᒪᓗ ᐊᖃᐃᖅ ᓄᐊᑲᐅᒪ ᒃᒍ ᓓᐸᖄ.) ᐃᒪᓕᒍᔾ ᐊᕐᐅᐅᔾᓂᑦ ᐅᐅᒪᑕ I970

Man trying to catch a goose.
Stone cut, 1964

ᐊᒍᐅᓂᑦ ᓄᖅᓗᓇᐊᑐᑦ ᐅᔾᕐᒡᕐᐱ ᐅᐅᑕ, I964

Felt pen, 1970

Stone cut, 1964

and then my parents would tell me to run up behind it, hooting and shouting, and put my foot on its neck. I'd run and I'd catch the goose and I'd stand there waving my arms like a bird. Sometimes we'd all have headaches from shouting and yelling.

In 'isha', the season when the geese lose their feathers, they are very easy to catch. They can't fly then and you can catch them easily on the grass. Just before I was born they used to drive the moulting geese into stone pens, but we didn't bother with pens. Geese are best found in mossy areas. Their feet are very sensitive and they won't go on the rocks. They always go where it's mossy or where there's grass.

Sometimes an Eskimo man will take a long rope with a loop on the end and place the loop on the ground. Then the Eskimo man will hide behind a rock and, when a goose passes over the loop, he'll pull the rope and he catches the goose.

ᓂᑦᒪᒃᕐᐸᑦᐊᑐᑦ ᑕᐅᒪ ᐊᑦᑦᒡᓄ ᐅᑲᐅᓇᕐᐱᐊᑦᐅᑐᒪ ᐅᓓᒃᕐᐅ ᕐᒪ ᐅᒪᑦᓇᕐ, ᓂᐱᖅᐅᔾᓄᒪ ᑲᐃᒪᓓᓇᑐᓄ ᑐᑕᒪᒍ ᑯᕐᕐᓕᒍᑦ ᐅᓓᕐᐸᑐᑦᐅᒪ ᓂᑦᕐᒃ ᓇᒍᕐᒪᓕᕐᒪ ᐃᒪᓓᓇ ᐊᕐᒍᐃᐋᕐᕐᒪ ᓴᕐᕐᒪ. ᐃᑕ ᓂᑦᑕᐅᕐᒪᓕᒪᒪ. ᐃᒪᓂᑐᑦ ᓂᐊᒍᒍᕐᐱᐊᑐᒪ ᓂᐱᖅᐅᖄᓇᓄᐅᒍ ᑲᐃᒪᓓᓇᖄᓇᓄᐅᒍᓄ.

ᐃᔾᐅᓇᒍ ᓂᑦᑦ ᐃᔾᐲᐃᔾᕐᐱᓓᓇᒍ, ᓄᒃᖅᐅᓂᕐᓇᐅᐊᐱᑦ. ᓄᕐᓇᐃᔾᕐᒪᓕᑕ ᑕᐅᒪ ᓄᒍᐅᖅᐅᓄᕐᓇᐅᐅ ᓄᐊᖅᕐᒪ. ᐃᐅᕐᒪ ᓅᐊᖄᐱᓄᐅ ᐃᐅᐱᑦ ᐃᕐᓄ ᐅᐱᖅᐱ ᐃᐅᐊᓄᐱᒃᔾᐱᓄ ᐃᑕ ᒃᒪᖅᐊᑕᐅᕐᒪᑐᒪ ᐃᐅᐊᓇᐱᓂᒃ. ᓂᕐᓂ ᑕᖅᓕᖅᐅᓂᒍᐊᓄᒃ ᓄᐊᕐᓕᒃᒪ. ᐃᕐᒪᒪ ᑕᕐᒍᐊᐊᕐᓄᐃ ᐊᒪᓗ ᐅᕐᓕᖅᐅᓇᓄᐅᓓᐱ. ᑕᐅᒪ ᓄᐊᒪᕐᓄᒍᕐ ᐅᕐᓄ ᓄᑐᐃᐊᓓᒍ.

ᐃᐅᓂᒍ ᐃᓄᕐ ᐊᒍᓇᕐ ᐊᕐᕐᐊᒪᓂ ᓄᕐᕐᕐᐊᑐᕐᕐ ᑕᕐᕐᓄᒍ ᐊᕐᕐᐊᓇ ᕐᓄᕐᑲᓄᒍ ᑕᐅᒪ ᕐᓄᒪ ᓄᐊᒍᕐᒍ. ᑕᐅᒪ ᑕᓄᕐᒪᓓᒪ ᒪᕐᓄ ᐅᖅᖅᐊᑦ ᐊᒪᓄ ᑕᐅᒪ ᓂᑦᒃ ᕐᓄᒪᑦ ᓇᓓᒪᑐᐊᒪᑦ ᐊᕐᕐᐊᒪ ᓄᕐᐃᓓᕐᓄ ᑕᐅᒪᒃ ᓄᒃᓓᕐᐱᐊᑐᑦ.

Flower spirit.
Engraving, 1968

ᐱᑐᔐᖅ
ᐅᑯᑭᕴᕐ ᑎᑎᑐᒪ, 1968

It's fun to chase a goose and it's always fun to be around animals – they are meat.

I can't remember the first time I tasted the white man's food, but I do remember one incident. At the time, they were building the Hudson's Bay post's big warehouse and I was just a little girl. I remember watching people unload the supply boat, and I was crying very hard. They gave me a pilot biscuit and I really liked it.

I like the white man's food but I think the old food was better for Eskimos. In the old days we had more food from animals and we didn't get sick so much. We ate the food raw. We used to eat seal, whale, caribou, ducks and ptarmigan all raw, though we used to cook the goose, and goose cooked is very good. We also used to cook the polar bear, though some people ate it raw.

We had fruit in the summer. We used to pick the berries on the tundra, and something else we ate was dulse. We

ᔑᐱᐊᓗ ᐅᑲᑭᑎᐊᖅ ᓂᓪᒥᑉ ᐊᒪ ᑕᐃᒪ ᔑᐱᐊᓗᑐᓂ
ᐅᒪᔑᑉᒥᐸᑏ -- ᐅᒪᔑᐊᑦ ᓂᑭᐅᒪᑕ.

ᐊᐅᑲᔐᑐᒪ ᑲᒪ ᔐᐅᑲᐸᒥ ᑲᓄ ᓂᑭᒪᓂ ᐅᑐᓂᒪᒪᒪ ᐃᑭ
ᐊᐅᑲᔐᕽᒪ ᐊᑕᐅᔭᒥ ᐅᑐᔑᒪ. ᑕᐊᒪᓗᐅᑎᓄᒍ ᐃᑭ ᓄᑕᐅᑐ
ᔑᒪᕽ ᓂᐅᐱᐊᑯ ᑭᑐᐃᓇᑭᐅᑎᓘᓂᓄ ᐊᒪᓗ ᑕᐊᒪᓗᓂ ᓄᐃᐊ
ᔑᐊᑐᓗᓘ ᐃᓇᐅᑐᐅᑎᓘᒪᔑᒪ. ᐊᐅᑲᔐᕽᒪ ᑕᑲᓇᐅᑎᓂᒪ ᐃᓄᖅᑭ
ᐅᓄᑕᑐᓂ ᐅᑎᐊᑦ ᐅᔑᒪᓂ ᐊᒪᓗ ᑭᐊᑲᐅᓘᔑᒪᒪ ᐊᕽᐊᓘ.
ᐊᐃᑐᑕᐅᑲᐅᔑᒪᔑᒪ ᔐᔑᑲᐅᒥ (ᑲᑯᔐᒥ) ᔑᓇᔐᕽ ᐱᐅᑭᐊᐅ
ᔑᓗᔐ ᐊᕽᔐᒪᕽ.

ᑲᓄᐊᑦ ᓂᑭᓂᒥᑭ ᐱᐅᕽᑐᒪ ᐃᑭ ᐅᔑᐊᓗᓂᓄᑭᕽ ᓂᑭᒪᕽ
ᐱᐅᓂᕽᐅᕽᐊᑎᔐᐅᑐᒪ ᐃᓄᖅᑦ. ᐅᔑᐊᑐᑎᓘᒍ ᓂᑭᑲᕽᐅᔐᐊ
ᑕᐅᔐᕽᒍ ᐅᒪᔐᐊᓄ, ᑲᓄᒪᔑᐊᑐᐅᑐᓘᖅᑦᑕ. ᓂᑎᐊᑐᑐᒍ
ᑲᑲᒪᑎᓘᒥ ᓂᑭᒥ.ᓂᑎᐊᑐᑐᒍ ᐊᔑᒥ ᑭᑐᓘᒥ, ᑐᐅᐱᓂᒥ,
ᓂᒪᐊᓄ ᐊᑎᓂᓗ ᐃᔑᓇᑏ ᑲᑲᓪᒪᓂᕽ ᐊᓘᕽᑲᐅᔑᓘᔐᐅᑐᒍ
ᓂᓪᒥ, ᐊᒪᓗ ᓂᑭ ᐊᓘᔑᒪᓂ ᐱᐅᔐᐊᓗ. ᐊᓘᕽᑲᐅᑎᔑᐊᑦ
ᐊᐅᐱᓂᒥᕽ, ᐃᓄᐊᑦ ᐃᑕᑎ ᒥᑭᕽᐸᐅᑐᕮᓘᒪᕽᓗ.

Eskimo camp scene.
Engraving, 1967

ᑐᐱᑲᐱᒃ
ᐅᑯᔭᕐᑲᕐᒥ ᓐᑕᑐᒪ, I967

used to hunt for dulse around the beaches. Sometimes, when the men went hunting, they would bring back dulse for the women. Eskimo people believe that it has some medicine in it; when they are sick they feel better if they have some.

Sometimes in the winter it was boring in the igloo but we never stayed inside much. We had warmer clothes in those days and it used to be fun when It was windy. The fathers would make toy sleds for their sons and daughters to slide on and, when the children had their sleds and their toy whips, they would play outside most of the day. Now they are in school all day and they have the habit of staying indoors.

Very often in those days when we felt happy in camp, Ashoona and I would play the accordion. My favourite brother once gave me an accordion and we both could play. The little children would come and dance. Kaka used to dance a lot.

ᐸᐅᒪᑲᐸᑲᐳᕐᐸ ᐊᐳᕐᑯ . ᐸᐅᒪᑕᑲᐳᐃᐸᔪ ᓄᒪᕐ, ᐊᒪᓗ ᐊᕐᕐᓄ ᓄᓐᕐᑲᑲᐳᕐᐸᔪᑦ ᑭᒃᐊᓄ. ᑭᒃᐊᐳᐸᑲᐳᑐᔪ ᕐᕐᒪ. ᐃᓗᓄ, ᐊᒍᓐᑦ ᐊᒍᓄᐊᑐᐃᓄ ᐊᓄᑕᐸᕐᕐᑲᑲᐳᐸᔪ ᑭᒃᐊᓄᑃ ᐊᑳᓄᐃ ᓄᓇᒃᕐᕐᓄ. ᐃᓄᐃ ᐊᓄᐊᕐᐸᐅᓐᑳᑐᓄᕐᒪ ᑭᒃᐊᕐ; ᑲᓄᓚᑐᐊᒪᕐ ᐊᑭᐸᑲᐳᐸᔪ ᓄᓐᐊᒪᕐ ᑭᒃᐊᕐ.

ᐃᓄ ᐅᑭᐅᕐ ᐊᑭᐊᓄᐸᑲᐳ ᐊᑭ ᑐᐊᒪᕐ ᐃᓄ ᐃᓄᐊᓄᕐᓄᐸᑲ ᐅᕐᓐᑐᔪᑦ. ᐅᑯᓄᑲᓄᑖ ᐊᓄᕐᑲᐸᑲᐳᒪᑕ ᑕᐊᕐᒪᓄ ᐊᒪᓗ ᑯᓄᐊᓄᐸᑲᐳ ᐊᓄᓐᕐᓚᐊᒪᒪ. ᐊᑕᑯᑐᕐᑦ ᐱᒍᐊᐳᐸᑲᐳᕐᕐᑦ ᑲᑐᓄᒍᐊᑕᐳᕐᓐ ᐊᑳᓄᕐᓄ ᐸᓄᕐᓄᓄ ᕐᐳᑕᐅᓐᕐᓄᓄ ᐱᐊᑕᒪᑦ ᑲᑐᓐᑲᓚᕐᑲᑐᕐᑦ ᐃᐃᑕᐳᓄᒍᐊᓄᓯᕐ, ᐱᒍᐊᑲᐳᐸᔪᑦ ᕐᓄᒪ ᐅᑲᓄᓚᑲᕐᑦ. ᒪᓄᑕ ᐃᓄᑐᐊᓄᕐᒪ ᐊᑲᓄᕐᒍᒪᐊᑕᓐᔪᓐᑦ.

ᑯᐊᐊᑕᕐᑲᕐᑦ ᓄᒪᓄ ᐊᑳᓄᕐᓄ ᓄᑲᓐᐱᕐᐸᑲᐳᐸᔪ ᑕᕐᐸᐊᒪᕐ. ᐊᓄᓇᕐᐳᑦ ᐊᐊᐳᑐᑕᑕᐳᐳᕐᒍᐸᑕ ᑕᕐᐸᐊᒪᕐ ᓄᕐᐳᓐᑦ ᑕᓚᓄᑲᕐ ᓄᕐᐳᒍᓄᐸᓐᒍ. ᐱᐱᓐᑲᑐᓄᐊᑦ ᑲᐊᐸᑲᐳᐸᔪ ᑕᓄᐱᓐᐊᐳᐸᓐᑦ. ᑲᑲ ᑕᓄᐱᕐᒪᓐᑕᐳᓄᐸᑲᐳᐸᔪᑦ.

Women would row the sealskin boats; men would go in the kayaks.
Coloured pencil and felt pen, ca. 1967

ᐊᒃᓇᐃᑦ ᑭᓯᒥ ᐅᒥᐊᑐᐸᓚᐅᑐ; ᐊᖑᑎ ᑲᔭᑐᑎᓗᒋ ᑕᒃᓴᓚᓄ ᐊᓚᐅᑎᓄᑦ ᐊᒪᓗ ᐃᒪᓕᒧ ᑎᑎᑐᓕ, I967 ᐅᑎᓗᒧ

Sometimes, just for two seconds, I could keep three stones up.
Felt pen, 1970

ᐃᓚᓕᓂ ᑭᑕᑯᓗ ᐊᑯᓂᐅᒋᑐᒃ ᐅᔭᕋᓂᒃ ᐱᓕᓯᓂ ᐃᓗᑭᑕᓗᓕ ᑲᓕᑕᑎᓯᒧᓇᐸᓚᐅᑐ ᓕ ᐃᒪᓕᒧ ᐊᓚᐅᑎᒧ ᑎᑎᑐᓕ, I970

Ashoona used to like to juggle. He could keep three small stones in the air and sometimes, just for two seconds, I could keep three stones up there, too.

ᐊᒃᓯᓇ ᐃᒃᓗᑭᑕᑎᐊᓴ ᐱᐅᓴᐸᓚᐅᔭᔭ. ᐱᓕᓯᓂᒃ ᐅᔭᕋᐱᓂ ᑲᓕᑕᑎᓯᒧᓇᐸᓚᐅᑐᒃ ᐃᓚᓂᓗ ᒪᕈᕕᑲᓚᐱᓯᒋ ᐱᓕᓯᓄᑕᐅᒃ ᐃᒃᓗᑭᑕᒧᓇᒥᔭᓕ.

We played lots of games. One game was 'illupik' – jumping over the 'avatuk', the sealskin float that hunters used to tie to the harpoons so the seals would stay on the water after they were killed. I hear young people in Cape Dorset still try to jump the avatuk at the youth club meetings.

ᐊᒥᓯᐊᓗᓂ ᐱᒧᐊᕈᓯᑲᐸᓚᐅᑐ. ᐊᑕᐅᓯ ᐱᒧᐊᕈᓯ ᐃᓗᐱ -- ᐊᕙᑕᐅᐸ ᑲᓕᓄᑦ ᒥᓯᑕᓯᓂ, ᐊᕙᑕᒥᒃ ᐊᒧᓇᓯᐊᑎ ᐳᕕᓯᐸᓚ ᐅᔭᔭ ᑭᓚᓚᓕᓯᒧ ᐅᓇᒧᑦ ᑕᐃᒪ ᓇᓯᒃ ᑭᕕᓂᐊᒋᒪ ᓄᑯᑕᐅᓯ ᒪᓕᓗᓂ. ᑐᓴᓚᐅᑐᓕ ᐅᕕᑲᐃᑦ ᑭᓕᓂ ᓯᓕ ᒥᓯᑕᕋᓯᑎᓗᒋᑦ ᐊᕙᑕᒧᑦ ᐅᕕᑲᐃ ᑲᑎᒪᑎᓗᒋ. ᐊᓯᓕᑕᐅᒃ ᐱᒧᐊᕈᓯᒃ ᐃᓄᐸ ᐊᒃᓴᓕ: ᐃᒪᓇᑕᓕ ᐱᒧᐊᐸᓚᐅᑐᒧᑦ ᑕᓯᒥᓕ ᐱᒧᐊᕈᓯᒥ --

Another game was the Eskimo tennis! This is how we played this game – we threw a ball underhand and tried to catch it in a sealskin racket. The racket was called an 'autuk'. We made the ball from caribou skin and stuffed it with something. We used to play this game a lot, even in winter. It was a good game, but they don't play it now; they are following the world.

ᐃᒋᑲᑕᓯᒧ ᐊᒃᓴ ᐊᓕᐅᐸ ᐊᑕᒧ ᐊᑯᓕᓯᑲᑕᓯᒧ ᓇᓯᐅᐸ ᑭᓯᓕ ᐊᒃᓴ. ᑕᓇ ᐊᒃᓴ ᑕᐃᔭᐅᕙᓚᐅᑐ ᐊᐅᑕᒥ. ᐊᒃᓴᓚᐅ ᐸᓚᐅᑐᒧᑦ ᐊᐅᑕᓚᐅᐸᓚᐅᑐᒧ ᑐᑐᐸ ᑭᓯᓕᓂ ᐃᓗᐊᒧᓗ ᐱᑕᓯ ᑐᓯᒧ ᑭᓯᑐᐃᓇᒥᒃ. ᑕᓇ ᐱᒧᐊᒋᓇᐸᓚᐅᔭᔭᕗᑦ ᑕᐃᒪᓕᑦ, ᐅᑭᐅᓕᓴᒥ ᐱᒧᐊᒧᕙᓚᐅᔭᔭ ᐃᓚ ᒪᓇ ᐱᒧᐊᑎᕙᔭᒧᓇᐃᑕᓕ, ᒪᓕᓕᕋᒥᒃ ᓯᓚᔭᐊᒥᒃ.

It was always most joyful when people came together in Cape Dorset. Every year we would make three trips to

ᑕᐃᒪᓕᓕᒪ ᑯᕕᐊᓇᐸᓚᐅᔭᔭᒃ ᐃᓄᐃᑦ ᑎᑭᐅᑲᓕᒪᑕ ᑭᓕᓄᑦ. ᐊᕋᒧᑕᒪ ᐱᓕᓯᕕᓯᑕ ᐊᐅᓚᐸᓚᐅᑐᒧ ᑭᓕᓕᐊᓯᑕ ᑭᒧᓯᑯᑦ.

One game we played was 'illupik' –
jumping over the sealskin float.
Felt pen, 1970

ᐱᒍᐊᐸᓚᐅᑕᑕ ᐃᓚᓚ ᐃᓗᐱᒃ ᒥᓯᑲᑕᓯ
ᑕ ᐊᕙᑕᒧ ᐃᒪᓕᒧᑦ ᐊᓚᐅᑎᒧ ᑎᑎᑐᓚ
I970

Cape Dorset with the dog team. When the nights were light we would travel after midnight and build an igloo when we stopped. It used to be cold when it was windy! We would go to Dorset to sell the fox skins to the Bay and get supplies. We got good prices for the fox then; fox used to be worth a lot. We would buy in exchange what we call the grub – the white man's food – tea, flour, salt, baking powder and shortening.

We always made one trip in summer to see the Nascopie. This ship used to bring all the supplies for the year to the Bay. We were always happy to see the Nascopie. One year the Nascopie went on some rocks coming into Dorset and was wrecked. Many people got things from the wreckage. I remember my son, Kiawat, got a primus stove and some blankets. He saw other people getting things and decided he should have something, too.

In those days, a lot of people and families would spend a long summer in Cape Dorset and then, before the weather

ᐅᓄᐊᒥ ᑕᑐᒍᓇᐃᑐᐊᒪᑦ ᐊᐅᓚᐸᓚᐅᑐᒍ ᑭᑎᕋᕆᓯᒪᓕᑎᓗᒍ
ᐅᓄᐊᓚ ᐃᓗᕕᓚᓕᐅᐸᓯᑕ ᓄᑲᑲᑕ. ᑭᐅᓇᐸᓚᐅᔪᔪ ᐊᓄᕆᓕᒪ!
ᑭᓚᓕᐊᐸᓚᐅᑐᒍ ᓂᐅᕈᑎᑲᕆᐊᑐᓯᑕ ᑎᕆᓚᓂᐊᔭᓂ ᓂᐅᕕᑎᑯᓄᑦ
ᓂᐅᕕᑎᐊᑐᓯᑕᓗ ᓂᐅᕕᐊᓴᒥᒃ. ᐊᑭᑲᓯᐊᑲᑯᔭᐅᕙᓚᐅᕋᑕ
ᑎᕆᓚᓂᐊᔭᓂᒃ ᑕᐃᓯᒪᓂ, ᑎᕆᓚᓂᐊᔭᑦ ᐊᑭᑐᔪᐊᓗᕙᓚᐅᔪᒪ.
ᓂᐅᕕᐸᓚᐅᑐᒍ ᓂᐅᕕᐅᑎᑲᓯᑕ ᑕᑯᓂᓚᐅᓂᕋᑕᑎᓂ -- ᑲᓗᓇᑦ
ᓂᑭᓚᓂ ᑎᒥ, ᐸᓚᐅᓚᒥ, ᑕᕆᐅᒥ, ᐳᔪᓴᐅᑎᒥ ᐳᓂᒥᓗ.

ᐊᐅᓚᐸᓚᐅᑐᒍ ᐊᑕᐅᓯᐊᓯᑕ ᐊᐅᔭᑯᑦ ᑕᑯᔭᑐᓯᑕ ᓇᓯᑯᐱᒥ.
ᑕᓇ ᐅᒥᐊᔪᐊᒃ ᓂᐅᕕᐊᓴᓕᒪᓂᒃ ᑎᑭᐅᕈᕙᓚᐅᔪᒪᑦ ᐊᕋᒍᒪᑦ
ᓇᒪᑐᓴᓂ ᓂᐅᕕᕕᒧ. ᑯᕕᐊᓯᐸᓚᐅᑐᒍ ᑕᑯᕆᐊᓴ ᓇᓯᑯᐱᒥ.
ᐊᑕᐅᓯᒥ ᐊᕋᒍᒥ ᓇᓯᑯᐱ ᐅᔭᕋᑯᓚᐅᓯᒪᒪ ᑲᐃᓚᓯᓯᓂ ᑭᓚᓄ
ᑕᐃᒪ ᓯᕋᓚᐅᓯᒪᒪ. ᐊᒥᓯ ᐃᓄᐃ ᐱᑕᓚᐅᓯᒪᔪ ᑭᓯᑐᐃᓇᓂ
ᓯᕋᓂᑯᕕᓂᓂᒃ ᐃᑲᑎᓂᑯᕕᓂᓂ. ᐊᐅᓚᕈᔪᓚ ᐃᒃᓂᓚ ᑭᐅᓚᒃ,
ᓯᐳᔪᑕᑎᓗᒍ ᑭᐱᓂᓗ. ᑕᑯᓂᓚᒥ ᐃᓄᑲᑎᕆ ᑭᓯᑐᐃᓇᑕᑎᓗᕆ
ᑕᐃᒪ ᐃᓯᒪᓯᔪᕕᓂ ᐱᕆᐊᑲᒥᓚᒥᑕᐅᒃ.

ᑕᐃᓯᒪᓂᐅᑎᓗᒍ ᐊᒥᓯᐊᓗᐃ ᐃᓄᐃᑦ ᑭᑐᓚᑎᓗ ᐊᐅᔭᑲᓕᒪ
ᑭᓚᓂᐸᓚᐅᑐᑦ ᐊᒪᓗ ᑕᐃᒪ ᓯᓚᓚ ᑭᐅᓇᓯᕆᓂᓚᓂ, ᓄᑕᒥᒃ
ᑐᐱᕕᓴᓯᐅᐸᓚᐅᑐᑦ ᓄᓇᒥ. ᑯᕕᐊᓯᐸᓚᐅᑐᒍ ᑲᑎᒪᓕᕋᐃᓚᑕ.

In the old days there were good dancers.
Felt pen, 1970

ᐅᕙᓯᐊᕈᑎᓗᒍ ᑕᓂᓯᓯᐊᐸᓚᐅᑐᑦ
ᐃᒪᓕᒧ ᐊᓚᐅᑎᒧᑦ ᑎᑎᑐᒐ, 1970

got cold, they would look for new camps inland. We used to be happy to be together. There would be dances at the Bay residence and at the warehouse. I only danced when I moved into the settlement after my husband died, but there were many people in Cape Dorset then who were good dancers. I don't remember the drum dances; I only remember the accordion dance. They danced Eskimo dances that went on for a long time – there were no drunks in the dances then!

This was the old Eskimo way of life; you couldn't give up because it was the only way. Today I like living in a house that is always warm but, sometimes, I want to move and go to the camps where I have been. The old life was a hard life but it was good. It was happy.

My husband died at Natsilik. That year I hadn't wanted to go to Natsilik and neither had Namoonie. But Ashoona begged us to go and so we did. The week my husband became sick we heard that his brother had died in Cape

ᑕᓂᓯᐸᓚᐅᒪᑕ ᓂᐅᕕᑎᑯ ᐃᒃ ᓗᒐᓂ ᐊᒪᓗ ᑭᓯᑐᐃᓇᑯᕕᒥ ᑕᓂᓯᐸᓯᑎ. ᑕᓂᓯᓯᒪᔭᒐ ᑭᓯᐊᓂ ᓄᓯᒪᓕᕋᒪ ᐃᒃᓗᒃᑐᒧᑦ ᐅᐃᒐ ᑐᑯᒐᓕᑎᓗᒍ, ᐃᓚ ᐊᒥᕆᓂ ᐃᓄᓂ ᑭᒐᓂ ᑕᓂᓯᓯᑎᑲᐸ ᓚᐅᑐᒃ. ᐊᐅᓚᕗᔭᕆᑐᒐ ᐊᓇᐅᓕᒐᒧ ᑕᓂᓯᑐᓂ ᒧᒥᑐᓂᒃ; ᐊᐅᓚᕗᔦᒐ ᑭᓯᐊᓂ ᑕᓯᔦᐊᒧ ᑕᓂᓯᑐᓂ. ᑕᓂᓯᐸᓚᐅᑐ ᐃᓄᐃ ᑕᓂᓯᕈᓯᕆᓂ ᐊᑯᓂ ᓄᑲᓯᒍᒐᑎ -- ᐃᒥᐊᓗᓯᒪᔦᑲᔭᑎᓇᒍ ᒧᒥᑐᓂᒃ ᑕᐃᓯᒪᓂ!

ᑕᓇ ᐃᓄᐃ ᐅᕙᓯᐊᕈ ᐱᐅᓯᑎᕙᓚᐅᑕᒐ ᓴᐱᑎᓇᔭᕆᑐ ᑕᐃᒪᓇ ᑭᓯᐊᓂᐅᕙᓚᐅᒪᑦ. ᒪᓇᓕ ᐱᐅᓴᑐᒐ ᐃᒃᓗᒥᕆᐊᓴ ᑕᐃᒪᒐᑦ ᐅᑯᔦᑐᐃᓇᐅᒪ ᐃᓚ, ᐃᓚᓂᑯ ᓄᒍᒪᕙᑐᒐ ᑐᐱᓯᒪᕆᐊᑐᓗᒐ ᓄᓇᕆᕙᓚᐅᑕᑎᓄ. ᐃᓄᓯᑐᒃ ᐊᒃᐅᕙᓚᐅᕆᑐ ᐃᓚ ᐱᐅᕙᓚᐅᑐ. ᑯᕕᐊᓇᐸᓚᐅᒐᒥ.

ᐅᐃᒐ ᓇᓯᓕᒥ ᑐᑯᓚᐅᓯᒪᒪ. ᑕᓇ ᑐᑯᕕᒐ ᐊᕋᒍᑎᓗᒍ ᓇᓯᓕ ᒧᒍᒪᓚᐅᓯᒪᕆᑐᒐ ᐊᒪᓗ ᑕᓇ ᓇᒧᓇᐃ ᑕᕗᒐᒍᒪᓚᐅᓯᒪᕆᒥᔦ. ᐃᓚ ᐊᒃᓯᓇᑉ ᑕᕗᒐᑯᓚᐅᓯᒪᒪᑎᒍᑦ, ᑕᕗᒐᓚᐅᓯᒪᔦᒍᑦ. ᑕᕙᓂᓴᐃᓇ ᐅᐃᒪ ᑲᓂᒪᕕᕆᓚᐅᑕᒐᓂ ᐱᓇᓯᐊᕈᓯᒥ ᑐᓴᓚᐅᓯᒪ

Packing a sleigh (detail).
Coloured pencil and felt pen,
ca. 1967

ᑲᒍᖕᒥ ᐅᕆᓴᐅᔪ (ᐃᓚᐃᓕᓂᒥ)
ᑕᕐᓴᓂᐊ ᐊᒡᐱᓂᐊ ᐊᓚᐅ ᐃᓚᒍᖕᑦ
ᑎᑎᑐᒪ, I967 ᐅᑎᔪᐊ

Dorset, but we didn't tell Ashoona because we were afraid it would make him even sadder. He died of a very bad sickness. Many people died at that time in the camps and in Cape Dorset. There was no doctor then and nobody knew what the sickness was.

For a long time after Ashoona died we were very sad. Sometimes I thought I would lose my mind. Whenever a dog team came to the camp, Ottochie would go and look for his father. He thought he would find him.

In the spring after Ashoona died, we came out of Natsilik on a dog team. We came here to Cape Dorset just for a little while. But my relatives were no longer here. My eldest brother had died on the water; he was on a kayak and didn't return. My other brothers, with my mother who lived for a long time, had gone to Resolute Bay – some of them died around there just last year, I hear. Now I am the only one left and I often think that I will not live much longer, now that my relatives are all dead.

ᐊᒍᑦ ᓄᑲᑦ ᑐᑦᕆᐊᒪ ᑭᓕᓂ. ᐃᓪ ᐅᑲᐅᑎᓚᐅᕐᒪᕆᑦᑖᑦ
ᐊᑉᕐᓇᑉ ᑯᐊᐊᑯᕆᓪᐊᑐᐱᕐᑐ ᐊᓴᓂ ᐊᔪᑎᕐᔪ. ᑐᑯᓪᐅᕆᒪᕐᑉ ᐊᑉ
ᕆᐊᒍᑉ ᑲᓪᕆᓇ. ᐊᕐᕆᑦ ᐃᓄᐃ ᑐᑯᓪᐅᕆᔪ ᑖᕐᒪᓄ
ᓄᓇᓂ ᐊᒪᓗ ᑭᓕᓇ. ᓗᑕᑉᓴᓇᔪ ᐊᒪᓗ ᑲᐅᕆᒪᑉᓴᓇᔪ
ᑲ.ᓄᐊᑐᓂᒪᒪᑦ ᑲᓇᓗᑉ.

ᐊᑐᓄᐊᓗ ᐊᑉᕆᐊᑉ ᑐᒪᒐᓄᔪ ᑯᐊᒡᑦᕆᑐᐸᓗᑐᐱᕆᔪᒪ.
ᐃᓪᓂ ᐊᕆᓚᐅᑉᔪᐸᑕᐅᑐᒪ. ᐆᑯᑐᑲᓚᐃᓪ ᑭᔪᕐᓄ ᓄᐋᓄ
ᐅᑲᐅᑐᖃ. ᓄᑲᕐᔪᑲᑎᒪ ᑭᓂᐸᓄᐅᑐᑉ ᐊᑉᑕᕐᓄᑉ. ᓇᓄᕐᐊᑐ
ᑐᑎᕐᓄ ᐊᑉᑕᕐᓄᑉ.

ᐊᑉ ᕆᓇ ᑐᒪᒐᓄᔪ ᐅᖢᕿᑯ ᐊᐅᑕᑐᐅᕐᒪᕐᔪ ᓇᓇᒥᓪᕆᑦ
ᑭᔪᕐᔪ. ᑭᑕᐱ ᑕᒪᐅᑲ ᐃᓂᓄᑐᐅᕆᒪᕐᔪ ᑭᓕᓇ. ᐃᓪ ᐃᓇᑉ
ᑕᒪᓄᔪᔪᐊᓄᑐᐅᕆᒪᕐ. ᐊᑐᒪ ᐊᑐᕐᕿ ᑐᑯᐅᕆᒪᕐ ᐊᓚᓂ;
ᑲᕐᑐᑐᓄ ᐅᑎᒐᑐᐅᕐᒪᕆᓂᑐᑉ. ᐊᕆᕐᓗ ᐊᓄᑉ, ᐊᓄᓄᓗ
ᐃᓄᕐᒪᕆᐊᑦ ᐊᑐᓂᕐᓗ, ᑲᐅᕆᐊᑐᔪᕐᒪᕐ ᓯᓗᕝᒍ ᐃᓄᕆᑦ
ᑐᑯᕐᓂᑐ ᑖᐃᓄᑎ ᐊᖢᓂᐊᓄᑉ, ᑐᓯᓂᐅᔪᒪ. ᒪᓇᑦ ᐊᕿᐊ
ᑐᑐᓚᐅᒪ ᐃᕿᓚᑲᑐᒪ ᐃᓄᓄᑲᓪᕆᕆᐊᖃᓄᑉ, ᒪᓇ ᐃᓇᑉ
ᐃᓄᓄᑎᑉ ᑐᑐᓚᐅᓪᑕ.

After Ashoona died we were very poor and sometimes
we would be out of oil for the kudlik. Things were given to
us by other people; we used to get oil from Oshaweetok.
We lived in camps near Cape Dorset and my eldest son,
Namoonie, did the hunting and sometimes Kaka helped.
But for a long time, we were very poor and often we were
hungry. We were poor until Sowmik and the government
houses came.

Before Jim Houston came to Cape Dorset we had the
people at the Bay who were here for the furs, and we were
grateful to have them and very pleased to be able
to get tea, sugar and flour. But I think Sowmik was the
first man to help the Eskimos. Ever since he came, the
Eskimo people have been able to find work. Here in Cape
Dorset they call him 'The Man'.

When Sowmik came to Cape Dorset we had moved into
the settlement and were living here in a snowhouse. This
is how we first met him. A boat was coming in from Lake

ᐊᐸ ᒥᓇᐃ ᐃᑐᓕᓴᐱᐧ ᐊᐸᒥᐊᐱ ᒥᑯᓱᐱᐪᒍ ᐃᓴᓪ
ᐅᐸᒥᐊᔨᓯᐪ ᑯᓕᔨ ᐅᐸᒥᐱᒥ. ᐊᐧᐪᓯᐅᓯᐪ ᐃᑐᐱᕒᕒᐃᔪ;
ᐅᐸᒥᓯᓯᓯᐪ ᐅᐱᐊᔨᒥ. ᐊᐸ ᓯᐸᐪᔨᒥᓴᐪ ᑭᒪ ᓴᓇᐊᓯᐧ,
ᐊᒪᓴ ᐊᒪᓴᐱᐸ ᐊᐸᓯᒪ ᓇᔨᓇ ᐊᔨᓯᓯᒥᓯᓯ ᑯᑳ ᐃᓴᓪ
ᐊᐸᓯᒪᓯᒥ. ᐃᓴ ᐅᐳᕒᐊᓯᓇᐊᐪ, ᓯᑯᓕᒪᐊᓯᐧᐱᔪᐪ
ᑭᒥᐊᓴ ᓴᐅᒥ ᑭᓴᓪᒪᐱ ᐊᐸ ᐱᒥ ᑎᐱᒪᓕ ᓯᑯᔨᓇᐃᑐᐪᔪᐪ.

ᓴᐅᒥᐸ ᑎᐱᐪᐅᓇᒪᔪ ᑭᓇᐱᐪ ᓇᐅᐱᐁᐪᑯᐪᔪᐪ ᑕᓕᓇᐱᓇ
ᑭᓇᐱᐪ ᑎᓕᓴᐊᐸᓇᓇ ᐊᒪᓴ ᑯᐱᓯᐪᐧᑯᓇᐃᐪᐃᐧᔪᐅᐪ ᑕᓕᓇᓪᑕ
ᓇᑯᓴᐱᐧᑯᓇᐃᐧᔪᐅᐪ ᑎᒍᐊᓇᐱᐪᓴᐧᑕ, ᑦᐱᒪ ᐧᓇᐅᓕᕒᓇ. ᐃᓴ
ᓴᐅᒪ ᓯᐳᒍᐧᐅᓇᐅᐱᑯᐪᑲ ᐊᐸᑕᓇᐊᓇᐪᐅᓇ ᐃᓇᓇ. ᑕᐊᓕᓇᓇ
ᓴᐅᒥᐸ ᑎᐱᐪᐅᐱᓕᓕᐪ, ᐃᓇᐊᐪ ᐊᐪᓴᐪᓇᐧᐱᐱᕒᓇᐪ. ᓇᒪ
ᑭᓕᕒᐅᐪᓇᐪ ᐃᓇᐱᓇ ᐊᔪᐱᑎᐱᐧᓴᑕᐅᐪᐱ.

ᑕᐊᓕᓇᓇ ᓴᐅᒥ ᑭᓇᐪᐅᓇᔪ ᓇᓇᐅᐱᓕᐪᔪ ᐊᐸᐪᔪᑕ ᐊᒪᓴ
ᐊᐸ ᓇᐊᓕᕒᐅᔪᓇᐅᐪᓕᐪᔪ. ᑕᐊᓇᐱᑕ ᑲᑎᕒᐊᓕᓇᐪᐅᐪᓕᐪᔪᐪ
ᓴᐅᒥᓇ. ᑕᐊᓕᓇᓇ ᐅᕒᐊ ᑎᐱᐪᐅᓇᔨᐪ ᑭᕒᐱᒥ ᐱᓯᓇ ᑕᐊᓇ
ᓇᐅᐱᐅᐱᓇᐅᐪᓕᐪᔪ ᐊᓕᐅᐪ ᓇᐊᓇᓇ ᑕᑯᓇᐪᐪᑕ ᑭᓇᓕᓇᓪᓇᐪ.

Bringing a gift.
Felt pen, ca. 1967

ᐊᐃᑐᑎᓴᒥᒃ ᓇᔭᓯᔪᒃ
ᐃᒪᓕᒍ ᐊᓚᐅᑎᒍ ᑎᑎᑐᒐ,
1967 ᐅᑎᓗᒍ

Harbour and we went over near the Bay to see who was on it. That was the first time I saw Sowmik. We didn't know he was coming in and we had never heard of him before but, immediately, he began to ask for carvings and sewing. After this visit he came often to Cape Dorset, and then he built his house and the government office.

At first, after Sowmik came, I did lots of sewing. I made parkas and duffel socks with designs. Lots of women began to work – any kind of women so long as they could sew. I used to embroider animals and all kinds of living things. But it was always $12 for a parka – even though it was hard to do.

Two winters – two years – after Jim came to live in Cape Dorset, he began to ask for drawings. Many people had been doing the drawings before I started. It was only just before Jim went away that I heard people were drawing to make money. I heard that Kiakshuk was drawing, and he was my very close relative – my mother's sister's son.

ᑕᐃᓯᒪᓂ ᑕᑯᕆᐊᒐᓕᓚᐅᓯᒪᔪᒐ ᓴᐅᒥᒥ. ᑲᐅᔨᒪᓚᐅᓯᒪᕆᑐᒐ ᑲᐃᓂᐊᒪᒪᒐ ᑐᓴᓚᐅᓯᒪᓇᒍ ᐃᓚ, ᐊᐱᕆᓴᐅᑎᕆᐊᐱᓚᐅᓯᒪᔪᒃ ᓴᓇᒍᐊᒐᓂ ᒥᓯᓯᒪᔪᓂᓗ. ᓂᐅᕈᕆᓯᒪᓕᒐᒥ ᑎᑭᓯᒍᓯᓚᐅᓯᒪᔪ ᑭᒐᖂᑦ ᐊᒪᓗ ᑕᐃᒪ ᐃᒃ ᓗᓕᐅᓚᐅᓯᒪᔪ ᐃᒃ ᓗᓴᒥᓂ ᐊᒪᓗ ᑲᐯᒪᑯᑦ ᑎᑎᕋᕖᒐᓂᒃ.

ᓯᕗᓕᐸᒥ, ᓴᐅᒥ ᑎᑭᑲᒥᐅᑎᓗᒍ, ᐊᒥᓯᐸᓗᓂᒃ ᒥᓯᓚᐅᓯᒪᔪᒐ. ᐊᑎᕆᓚᐅᓯᒐ ᐊᒪᓗ ᐊᑎᕆᓴᔭᓂ ᐊᓕᑎᓚᐅᓯᒐ ᑕᒃᓴᑲᑎᓗᕆᑦ. ᐊᒪᓗ ᐊᒃᓇᐃᑦ ᐊᒥᓯᑦ ᒥᒃᓯᑲᑕᒥᑎᓗᕆ -- ᑭᓇᑐᐃ ᓇᑯᑦ ᒥᒃᓯᕈᓇᑐᐊᕋᒥ. ᒥᒃᓯᑕᓂᒃ ᑕᒃᓴᓕᐅᑎᕙᓕᐅᑐᒐ ᑲᕝᐃᑐᑐᐃᓇᓂᒃ ᐅᒪᔪᒍᐊᓂᒃ. ᑕᐃᒪᒪᓕᒪᒃ ᐊᑎᕆᑦ ᒥᓯᓗᕆ $12-ᑕᓚᓂ ᐊᑭᑲᐸᓕᐅᑐᑦ -- ᐱᔭᑎᐊᑐᒪᓗᐊᕋᒥ.

ᐅᑭᐅᓂ ᒪᕉᓂᒃ ᓴᐅᒥ ᑭᒪᓂᓕᓯᓂ ᐊᐱᑎᓯᓕᐅᓯᒪᔪ ᐱᔪᒪᓯᓂ ᑎᑎᑐᔭᓯᒪᔪᓂᒃ. ᐊᒥᓯᐊᓗᐃᑦ ᐃᓄᐃ ᑎᑎᑐᔭᑲᑕᓕᓕᐅᓯᒪᔪᑦ ᐱᕆᐊᓕᐅᑎᓇᒪ. ᓴᐅᒥ ᐊᐅᓕᕆᓗᐊᕋᐱᑎᓗᒍ ᑐᓴᓕᐅᓯᒪᔪᒐ ᐃᓄᐃᑦ ᑎᑎᑐᔭᕆᐊᓴᕆ ᑭᓇᐅᔭᓕᐅᒍᑎᕆᓯᕆ. ᑐᓴᓕᐅᓯᒪᔪᒐ ᑭᐊᓯᒥ ᑎᑎᑐᔭᑐᒥ ᐊᒪᓗ ᑭᐊᓯ ᐃᓚᓗᑐᕆᓕᐅᓯᒪᔭᒐ ᐊᓇᓇᒪ ᓄᑲᒐᑕ ᐃᒃᓂᕆᒪᐅᒃ.

Night demons of sky and earth.
Stone cut, 1961

ᐅᓄᐊᖅᓄᑦ ᕿᓚ ᓄᓇ
ᐅᖅᑐᒥ ᑎᑎᖁᑎ, 1961

Perils of the sea traveller.
Stone cut, 1960

ᐃᒪᒃᑦ ᐊᑉᖕᓄ ᓇᕐᐊᓄᑦ
ᐅᖅᑐᒥ ᑎᑎᖁᑎ, 1960

Kiakshuk was drawing a lot and I wanted to do drawings, too, to make some money. I bought some paper myself and I think I made four small drawings. I think I drew little monsters. I meant the drawings to be animals but they turned out to be funny-looking because I had never done drawings before. I took these drawings to Jim's office. I was scared to go there at first but he gave me money – I think it was $20.

I began to think, maybe someday I can be like Kiakshuk. Maybe I will. Kiakshuk was working really hard on the prints when he died. He worked right up to the time he died. I am still doing the drawings and perhaps I will die like Kiakshuk, doing the drawings right up to the end.

Because Kiakshuk was a very old man, he did real real Eskimo drawings. He did it because he grew up that way, and I really liked the way he put the old Eskimo life on paper. I used to see Kiakshuk putting the shamans and spirits into his work on paper. Were the shamans useful in

ᑭᐊᕐ ᑎᑎᖁᕐᖁᐊᓗᕐᑲᐅᕐᒪᖅ ᑕᒪ ᑎᑎᖁᒪᒐᕐᑲᐅᒐᒪᖁᑕᖅ ᓇᐅᐅᕐᑲᐅᒥ ᓂᐅᐱᑎᕐᖁᒪᑦᑯ ᐸᐊᕐᒥ ᑕᒪ ᓯᑕᐅᑯᒐᓂ ᒥᕿᐊᕐ ᑎᑎᖁᕐᑲᐅᕐᒪᑦᑯ. ᑎᑎᖁᕐᑲᐅᕐᒪᒪᖁ ᑐᔪᐊᒐᖕᓄ. ᑎᑎᖁᕐᑲᖅ ᐅᒪᕐᑕᐊᕐᒥᕐᒥᓗᕐᕆᕐᑦ ᑕᓗ ᐱᐅᕐᑐᒐᐊᒥᕐᑲᐅ ᒥᕐᕐᑦ ᑎᑎᖁᕐᑲᐅᕐᒪᕐᒪᓄᑦ. ᑯᖁ ᑎᑎᖁᕐᐊᑦ ᓴᐅᕿᐅᑦ ᑎᑎᖁᐊᓗᓄᕐᑲᐅᕐᒥᖅᑫ ᖃᐱᖁᕐᑲᐅᕐᒪᒪᖁ ᓭᑕᓕᐊᕐ ᕐᓄᖕᒥ ᑕᒪ $20-ᑕᒥ ᖃᐅᕐᓴᐅᕐᑲᐅᕐᒪᕐᑦ.

ᐃᕐᒪᓂᐅᕐᑲᐅᕐᒪᕐᖁ, ᐃᒪᖕ ᖃᒪᐃᓇ ᑭᐊᖕᕐᑎᑐᒐᓇᒥᕐᐅᖁ. ᐃᒪᖕ ᖃᖕᑐᒥ. ᑭᐊᕐᖕ ᐊᖕᕐᐊᖕ ᐱᒥᕐᐊᑎᕐᒡᓂ ᑎᑎᖁᕐᖅ ᑐᖃᕐᑲᐅᕐᒪᕐ. ᐱᐊᕐᕐᑲᐅᕐᒪᕐ ᓄᖁᕐᑕᐅᕐᒪᒡᒥᓂ ᑐᖃᒡᑕᑕᐅᕐ. ᕐᐊ ᑎᑎᖁᕐᑲᐅᕐᖅᑲᑐᕐᒪ ᐃᒪᖕᑕᐅ ᑐᖃᕐᒡᒪᕐᖁ ᑭᐊᕐᓄᑦᖕᑦ, ᑎᑎᖁᕐᑲᐅᕐᓄ ᓄᒐᐃᐅ ᓃᖁᓄ.

ᑭᐊᕐᖕ ᐊᑐᐊᓄᕐᑲᐅᕐᒪᒥᒥ, ᐃᓄᖕᑎᑎᖁᓄᒥ ᑎᑎᖁᕐᐸᕐᑲᐅᕐᐅᖅ. ᑕᐃᒪᓇᐃᓄᐸᕐᑲᐅᕐᖅ ᑕᐃᒪᓇ ᐃᓄᖕᓂᒐᒥᕐ, ᐊᖕᕐᐅ ᐱᐅᕐᕐᑲᐊᕐ ᕐᑲᐅᕐᑲᖅ ᐃᓄᐊᖅ ᐃᓄᕐᑐᖕᑲᓂᕐ ᐸᐊᐸᕐᖁᕐᓄᖕ. ᑯᐊᕐᕐᑲᐅᕐᑐᖅ ᑭᐊᕐᖕ ᐃᑕᖕᑎᓄᖁ ᐊᖕᑐ ᑐᖕᓄᖁ ᐱᕐᕐᕐᒥᕐᓄ ᐸᐊᐸᕐᖁᑦ.

Happy family.
Engraving, 1963

ᐃᓚᒋᑦ ᑯᕕᐊᓱᑦ
ᐅᑯᓯᓴᔭᒥ ᑎᑎᑐᒐ, I963

any way? I don't know much about shamans because I don't like to think about them. Did the Anglican clergymen tell people not to be shamans? I have never heard of a single minister telling an Eskimo not to be a shaman. People just didn't like to give instructions to these powerful people.

Jim Houston told me to draw the old ways, and I've been drawing the old ways and the monsters ever since. We heard that Sowmik told the people to draw anything, in any shape, and to put a head and a face on it. He told the people that this drawing was very good. Some people saw the monsters, somewhere, some place, but I have never seen the monsters I draw. But I keep on drawing these things and, sometimes, when I take Terry a monster drawing, I say, "Perhaps when I die I'll see these monsters."

Terry Ryan came to Cape Dorset just before Jim went away. Terry, whom we call 'The Printer', came to run the

ᐊᒐᑯᐃᑦ ᐊᑐᑐᐸᓗᕙ ᑲᓄᑐᐃᓇ? ᑲᐅᔨᒪᒋᑐᒐ ᐊᒐᑯᐃᑦ ᒥᓴ ᓄᑦ ᐃᓱᒪᒋᒍᒪᔭᒋᓇᑭ. ᐊᔪᑭᑐᐃᔨ ᐅᑲᐅᑎᓚᐅᐸ ᐃᓄᓂᑉ ᐊᒐᑯᑯᔨᒐᓂ? ᑐᓴᓚᐅᓯᒪᒋᓯᐊᑐᒐ ᐊᔪᑭᑐᐃᔨ ᐅᑲᑎᓗᒍ ᑕᐃ ᒪ ᐃᓄᓂ ᐊᒐᑯᑯᔨᒐᓂ. ᐃᓄᓄ ᒪᓕᑕᐅᑯᔨᒋᑐᐃᓇᓚᐅᓯᒪᔪᑉ ᑕᑯᓂᒐ ᓯᒍᔪᓂ ᐃᓄᓂᑉ.

ᓴᐅᒥᐅᑉ ᐅᑲᐅᑎᓚᐅᓯᒪᔭᒐ ᑎᑎᑐᔭᑯᓗᓂᒐ ᐅᕿᔪᐊᕈᓂᑕᓂᑉ, ᑕᐃᒪ ᑎᑎᑐᔭᓯᒪᔪᒐ ᐅᕿᔪᐊᕈᓂᑕᓂ ᐊᒪᓗ ᑐᒐᓂ ᑕᐃᒪᒐᓂ. ᑐᓴᓚᐅᑐᒐ ᓴᐅᒥ ᐅᑲᐅᑎᔪᕕᓂᑉ ᐃᓄᓂᑉ ᑎᑎᑐᔭᑯᔨᓯᓂ ᑲᓄᐃᑐᑐᐃᓇᓂᑉ, ᑲᓄᑐᐃᓇ ᐊᑭᓯᒪᔪᓂ, ᐊᒪᓗ ᓂᐊᑯᒐ ᐃᓕᓗᒍ ᑭᓇᑲᑎᓗᒍᓗ. ᐅᑲᐅᑎᓚᐅᑐ ᐃᓄᓂᑉ ᑕᓇ ᓂᐊᑯᑲᑐᑉ ᑭᓇᑲᓯᓂᓗ ᑎᑎᑐᔭ ᐊᑉᓯᐊᓗ ᐱᐅᔪᐸᓗᓚᐅᑐ. ᐃᓄᐃᑦ ᐃᓚᒥ ᑕᑯᓚᐅᑐ ᑐᒐᓂ, ᓇᒥᑐᐃᓇ, ᓄᓇᒥ ᐃᓚ ᑕᑯᓚᐅᓯᒪᔭᒋᑕᓂᑉ ᑐᒐᓂ ᑎᑎᑐᔭᐸᑐᒐ. ᐃᓚ ᑎᑎᑐᔭᒋᓇᑲᑕᑐᒐ ᑕᑯᓂᒐ ᐊᒪᓗ ᐃᓚᓂᑯ ᑎᐅᑎᒧᓯᓕᒐᒪ ᑐᒐᓂ ᑎᑎᑐᔭᓯᒪᔪᓂ ᐅᑲᓗᒐ "ᐃᒪᑲ ᑐᑯᒍᒪ ᑕᑯᓚᑕᑲ ᑕᑯᐊ ᑐᒐᐃᑦ". ᑎᐅᑎ ᕋᐃᔭᓐ ᑭᒐᓄᓚᐅ

Co-op. The Co-op sends the carvings and prints to the
south, and it is owned by Eskimos. I don't know exactly
how it works but there is a board of directors who are
Eskimo. Terry gives out the pens and the papers for
drawing, and later when we bring him our work, he pays
for the drawings and carvings. I don't do drawings when
Terry has gone somewhere; when Terry's away I get
tired of waiting for him. A lot of people miss him when
he's away.

Since the Co-op began I have earned a lot of money with
my drawing. I get clothes from the drawings, and I earn
a living from paper. Because Ashoona, my husband
is dead I have to look after myself, and I am very grateful
for these papers – papers we tear so easily. Whenever
I am out of everything, I do some drawings and I take them
to Terry at the Co-op and he gives me money with which
I can buy clothes and tea and food for the family. He is
paying well. I am happy to have the money and I am glad
we have a Co-op.

ᔆᒪᔦ ᓴᐅᒥ ᐊᐳᓚᕐᒍᐊᕃᐊᕆᐱ. ᑎᐲ ᑲ ᐊᐱᕿᑕᐳ
ᑎᑎᑕᒪ ᑎᑉᓚᐅᕐᒪᔦ ᑯᐳᐊᕲᒥ ᑲᒪᕐᐊᑐᕐᓂ. ᑲ ᑯᐳᐊᕓ
ᐊᐳᓚᑎᑉᑲᑐ ᓴᓂᐳᓚᓂ ᑎᑎᑕᓚᓂᓂ ᑲᓇᓕᕲ ᓴᐊᓚᓂ, ᐊᓚᓗ
ᓇᕲᓂᕲᐳᓄᓂ ᐃᓄᐃᑦ. ᑲᐳᕲᒪᕐᐳᑎ ᑲᓇᕓ ᐱᕆᒎᓂᓂ ᐊᐁ
ᐊᓚᕃᑲᑐ ᐃᓄᓂ. ᑎᑎᑕ ᑐᓂᕲᑲᑐ ᑎᑎᕳᑎᓄᕃ ᕃᐁᕃᓄᓂ
ᑎᑎᑕᕲᐱᕲᓇ ᐊᓚᓗ ᐊᕃᓇᑲᕲᓇ ᑎᑎᑕᕲᓇ ᕃᓇᔍᐊᓚᓇ.
ᑎᑎᑕᕲᑲᑲᕲᕲᑐᓚ ᑎᑉᑎ ᐊᐱᓚᕃᓚᑲᓚᐃᓗ ᓇᔍᐃᓇ; ᑎᑉᑎ
ᐊᐱᓚᕃᓚᓴᐊᓚᕃ ᐅᑕᕿᔫᕃᕃᕃ. ᐃᓄᐃᕃ ᐊᕆᕲᓇ ᐱᕃᕃᐃᕲᐳ
ᔆᓚᑲᑐᕐ ᐊᐱᓚᕃᓚᓴᐊᓚᕃ.

ᑕᐅᓚᓇ ᑯᐳᐊᕃᐱᕃ ᐱᕆᐊᕲᕃᐳᕲᓚᓚᕃ ᕿᓇᐳᕲᕃᐳᕃᓛᕃ
ᑎᑎᑕᕲᑲᓂᕃ. ᐊᓚᕃᕃᕃᕃᓚ ᑎᑎᑕᕲᑲᓂᕃ, ᐊᓚᓗ ᕿᓇᐳᕲᓇᐳ
ᐃᓄᓚ ᐸᐃᕲᓇ. ᐅᑕᓚ ᑐᑐᓚᕃᓚ ᐊᕲᓂ ᑲᒪᕐᐊᕲᒪᓚ ᐊᓚᓗ
ᓇᕃᕲᑐᓚ ᑕᕲᓂᓚ ᐸᐃᕿᓂ ᐊᕃᕲᐊᕃᐱᕃᕲᓇ. ᑲᑐ ᐃᓇᕿᓚ
ᓄᔍᕆᕲᓚ ᕿᕃᑐᐃᓇᓂ, ᑎᑎᑕᕲᕃᕃᐳᓚ ᕃᐊᓚ ᑎᑉᑎᔍᕿᓚᕃᕃᕃ
ᑯᐳᐊᕃᔍᕃ ᕿᓇᐳᕲᓇ ᕿᐊᕃᕃᐳ ᐊᕲᕃᓂ ᓂᐳᐱᐳᑎᕿᕃᓇ ᑎᕃᕿ
ᐃᓚᕃᓇ ᓂᑎᕲᕃᕆ. ᑎᑉᑎ ᐊᕿᓚᕃᐊᕲᕃᔍᕃᐳ. ᑯᐊᐊᑐᓚ
ᕿᓇᐳᕲᕿᕃᐊᕃ ᐊᓚᓗ ᓇᕃᕲᑐᓚ ᑯᐳᐊᕃᕿᓚᕃ.

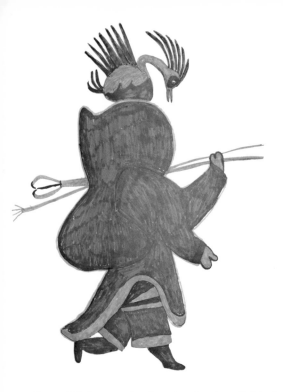

The woman with the blue fish spear.
Felt pen, 1970

ᐊᑉ ᐊᑉ ᑐᕈᕅᑦᒥᑉ ᑲᑉᕼᑕᑉ
ᐃᖃᓇᒍ ᐊᒡᐳᑎᒍᑦ ᑎᑎᒍᒪ, 1970

Pitseolaks.
Felt pen, 1970

ᐱᕈᐳᓐᑦ
ᐃᖃᓇᒍ ᐊᒡᐳᑎᒍᑦ ᑎᑎᒍᒪ, 1970

Does it take much planning to draw? Ahalona! It takes much thinking, and I think it is hard to think. It is hard like housework.

The other day I drew an Eskimo woman with a blue fish spear. I did not want to leave the fish spear alone; that is why I put the bird on her head. There's a baby hidden inside the parka, too – you can tell by the shape of the parka!

When I first started doing the drawings I did all the work in black and brown, and I still like these two colours, although now we are using many coloured pens. Jim said to draw the old ways in bright colours.

After Terry gets the drawings, some are put on the stone and made into prints. The drawings are carved into stone by Nawpachee's husband, Eegyvudluk, and by Iyola, Lukta and Ottochie. After they are put on the stone, they are always better. Sometimes we make prints, too, with

ᑎᑎᒍᔅᑕᒪᕆᒥᒐᕆ ᐱᕼᑎᐊᒍᐊᑉ! ᐊᑉᓄᐊ! ᒪᑎᐊᓴᑉ ᐊᑉᕆᐊᓴ.
ᐃᕐᒥᒐᐊᓴᕈ ᐳᕈᒪ ᐃᕐᒥᒐᐊᐸᓴᐊᓴᕆᐳᒪ. ᐱᕼᑎᐊᒍᐊᓴᕈ
ᐃᑉ ᓴᓄᕼᑎᐊᓐᑕᑦ.

ᐳᐊ ᐃᓴᓗᓇ ᑎᑎᒍᔅᓴᓴᐳᕆᒣᒪ ᐃᓴᒥ ᐊᑉᓴᒥ ᑐᕈᕅᐸᓇᒍ
ᐃᑉᓴᒥ ᑲᑉᕼᓴᑐᒥ. ᐊᑕᐳᕆᐳᓴᓴᐳᕆᓴᓇ ᐃᑉᓴᒥ ᑲᑉᕼᐸᑎ,
ᑕᐃᓴᐃᓴᓚᑦ ᓴᐊᑦᓴᓗᓴᕈᕆᐳᓴᓇᒪ ᑯᕼᓴᐸᐊᕼᑉ. ᐱᐊᔅᑯᓴᓴᕼᑉ
ᐃᓴᕈᓴᕈᐊᑉᓴᑐᑕᑉ ᐊᓄᕅᐳᑦ ᐃᓴᐊᓴ, ᑕᑯᕼᐳᔅ ᐊᑉᕈᓴᓄᓴᓇ
ᐊᓄᕅᐳᑦ !

ᕈᐳᓴᕈᕅᒥ, ᑎᑎᒍᔅᑲᓴᓴᐃᐸᕈᒪ ᑎᑎᑉᐳᔅᑲᑉ ᐃᓴᓇᑕᑉ
ᕅᓴᑕᐳᕈᓴᐳᔅᑦ ᑲᕈᓴᑎᓴ ᐊᒡᓴ ᕈᓴ ᑕᑯᕼ ᒪᕈ ᒥᒍᐊᑕᑉᕼ
ᐱᐳᕅᓴᕈᕼᑉ, ᒪᓇ ᐊᒥᕈᓴ ᐊᑐᓴᕈᓴᐊᑐᒪ ᑲᕼᕼᓴᓇᕼᑉ ᑎᑎᑐᔅ
ᐳᑎᓴᕼᑉ.

ᑎᐳᑎ ᐱᕈᕼᓚᓴᑐᐊᒪ ᑎᑎᒍᔅᕈᓴᕈᕼᓇ ᐃᓴ ᐳᕅᒍᑕᐳᕼᓴᑎ
ᐊᒡᓴ ᑎᑎᒍᔅᓴᑲᐊᓇᕅᐳᕼᑎ. ᑕᑯᕈ ᑎᑎᒍᔅᕈᓴᕈᓴ ᕼᓴᕼᕈᕈᓴᓴ
ᐳᕅᒍᓴ ᓴᑲᕈᐳᕼ ᐳᐊᓴᓇ, ᐃᓴᕈᓴᒍᓴ, ᐊᒡᓴ ᐊᐊᐳᓴᓴᒍᕼᑉ,
ᓴᑦᑲ ᐳᐳᑎᓴᒍᓴᕈ. ᑕᑯᕈ ᑎᑎᒍᔅᕈᓴᕈᓴᕈᑲᐳᑎᓴᒥᒍ ᑲᕼ ᕼᓇᕼᐳᕅᑎ
ᑲᑯᕈᓴᒍᓴᕈ ᐳᕅᒍᓴᑲᐳᕼᑲᓴᓚᒥ, ᑕᒪᓚᕈᓴᒪ ᐱᐳᓴᕈᐳᕼᑲᐳᕼᑉ.

Girl on a windy day.
Coloured pencil and felt pen,
ca. 1967

ᓂᕕᐊᓯᐊᒃ ᐊᓄᕆᓯᐅᑐᒃ
ᑕᒃᓴᓚᓄ ᐊᓚᐅᑎᓄ ᐊᒪᓗ ᐃᒪᓚᒧᑦ
ᑎᑎᑐᒐ, 1967 ᐅᑎᓗᒍ

stencils and with copper plates. Now some of the drawings are also arranged on material and, when it is carefully done, it looks very well.

Sometimes, when I see pictures in books of my drawings and prints, I laugh. I laugh to think they have become something. But even when they are waiting for papers from the south, Terry Ryan is giving artist's papers to me. Sometimes, when I am the only one who is given papers to draw on, I am scared that the other women will become jealous of me. Sometimes I feel sorry when other people don't have papers – papers which I can get.

But many Cape Dorset people have done well with the prints. I don't know who did the first print, but Kiakshuk, Niviaksiak, Oshaweetok and Tudlik were all drawing at the beginning. I liked the first prints – I liked them because they were truly Eskimo. Others have worked well, too. Parr was an old man when he began to draw, and he died last year, but I really loved the way he drew. Kenojuak

ᒪᓇ ᑎᑎᑐᔪᓯᒪᔭᐃ ᐃᓚᒋ ᐊᑭᑕᐅᓯᒪᒥᔭᑕᐅ ᑲᓗᓇᑕᒧ ᐊᒪᓗ ᐱᓯᐊᓯᒪᑐᐊᒐᒥ, ᐱᓯᐊᓯᒪᔭᐸᓗᑲᑕᑐᑦ.

ᐃᓚᓂ, ᑕᑯᒐᒪ ᐊᐳᒧᐊᓂ ᐅᑲᓚᒪᒐᒥᑐᓂ ᑎᑎᑐᔪᑕᕕᓂᓂᕙᒐ ᑎᑎᑐᔪᒧᓯᒪᔭᓂᓗ, ᐃᔭᐸᑐᒐ. ᐃᔭᐸᑐᒐ ᐃᓯᒪᓯᒐ ᑕᑯᐊ ᓯᓇᑐᐃᓇᒧᒋᐊᒋ. ᐃᓚ ᐅᑕᑭᑲᓗᐊᒪᑕ ᐸᐃᐸᓂ ᑲᓗᓇ ᓄᓇᒐᓂ ᐱᔭᓂ, ᑎᐅᕆᐅᑉ ᐊᐃᑐᐸᑕᒐ ᑎᑎᑐᔪᑎᐅᑉ ᐸᐃᐸᒐᓂ. ᐃᓚᓂ ᐅᕙᒐ ᑭᓯᐊᓂ ᐸᐃᐸᒥᒃ ᐊᐃᑐᑕᐅᔪᕋᐃᒐᒪ ᑎᑎᑐᔪᕕᓴᒥᒃ ᑲᐱᐊᓯᐸᑐᒐ ᐊᓯᑲ ᐊᒃᓇᐃ ᐱᐳᓗᓴᓴᓂᐊᒪᑕ ᐅᕙᓂ. ᐃᓚᓂ ᒪᒥᐊᐸᑐᒐ ᐊᓯᑲ ᐃᓄᐃᑦ ᐸᐃᐸᑲᒧᓇᐃᑐᐊᒪᑕ ᐸᐃᐸᒥ ᐅᕙᒐ ᐱᔭᓇᑕᒐᓂ.

ᐃᓚ ᐊᒥᓯ ᑭᒐᒥᐅ ᐃᓄᐃᑦ ᐱᓯᐊᓯᒪᔭᓂ ᑎᑎᑐᔪᓚᐅᓯᒪᔭᑦ. ᑲᐅᐳᒪᒋᑐᒐ ᑭᓇ ᓯᕗᓚᐸᐅᓯᓂ ᑎᑎᑐᔪᓯᒪᔭᓚᐅᓂᒪᒐ, ᐃᓚ ᑭᐊᓯ ᓂᕕᐊᓯᐊᒃ, ᐅᓯᐃᑐ ᑐᓚᓗ ᐃᓗᓇᑎᒃ ᑎᑎᑐᔪᓯᒪᔭᓚᒪ ᓯᕗᓚᒥ ᐱᒋᐊᒐᓯᑎ. ᐱᐅᓴᑐᒐ ᓯᕗᓚᒥ ᑎᑎᑐᔪᒧᓯᒪᑲᑐᕕᓂᓂ ᐱᐅᒋᔪᑲ ᐃᓄᓚᑎᐅᕙᓚᐅᒪᑕ. ᐊᓯᒋ ᐱᓯᐊᐸᓚᐅᒥᔭᐃᑕᐅᒃ. ᐸ ᐃᑐᐊᓗᓚᐅᑐ ᑎᑎᑐᔪᓚᓴᓯᓂ ᐊᒪᓗ ᑐᑯᓚᐅᑐ ᐊᕋᓂ, ᐃᓚ ᐱᐅᒋᔪᐸᓗᒋᓚᐅᑕᑲ ᑎᑎᑐᕋᒧᓯᒋᕙᓚᐅᑕᒐ. ᐊᒪᓗ ᑭᓄᐊᔭᐊᑉ ᐅᒃ ᐱᓚᐊᒐ ᑐᓴᓚᐅᑐᒐ ᐱᓇᑎᔪᐅᓯᔭᕕᓂᒥ ᑲᓗᓇ ᓄᓇᒐᓂ.

made the owl which, I hear, became famous in the south.
Lucy is good sometimes and I have seen something
of Pudlo's which I like.

My children are working for the Co-op, too. Kaka and
Kiawat are carving. Kiawat has also done prints – he once
drew a muskox with big horns – but he has been carving
since he was a young boy and is good at the carving.
Kaka also makes good money carving. Nawpachee does
sewing, drawing and carving, and Kumwartok and
Ottochie and Namoonie carve sometimes. But Kaka and
Kiawat are best. Once, Kiawat and Nawpachee's husband,
Eegyvudluk, went to Ottawa to do some carving and meet
the Queen. Jim Houston arranged it. But they didn't go
to Frobisher Bay to see her there when she came this year.
They had seen her already.

I know I have had an unusual life, being born in a skin tent
and living to hear on the radio that two men have landed
on the moon. I think the new times started for Eskimos

ᓄᕕᐅᑦ ᑎᑎᑐᖅᒪᒥᕐᑦ ᐱᐅᑕᕐᕌ, ᑕᑯᕐᒪᕌᒍ ᐱᒋᑐᐃᓇᕐᖅ
ᖁᓇᐅ ᑎᑎᑐᖅᑕᐊᓂᕐᓂᖅ ᐱᐅᕐᑕᕆᐅᕐᑲᓂᖅ, ᐊᒻᓗ ᐃᐅᖅᑐᒪ
ᒍᐊᓇᐊᓂ ᑎᑎᑐᖅᕐᒪᕌᓂᓗ ᑲᑲᐱᐅᑦ ᑎᑎᑐᖅᑲᓂᕐᓂᖅ.

ᑭᑐᒪᖅ ᐃᖃᓇᐊᕐᕌ ᑯᐅᐊᕐᒥ. ᑲᑲ, ᑭᑐᒪᑦᓚ ᖃᐅᐱᑐ.
ᑭᑐᒪᕐᑦ ᑎᑎᑐᖅᕐᒪᕌᒐᑐᐱᖅ ᐊᑐᕐᒪᕆᕐᖅ ᐊᑕᐅᕐᐊᑕᓂ ᑎᑎᑐ
ᖅᕐᒪᕐᖅ ᐅᕐᒪᔭᕐᖅ ᐊᕐᕌᒐᕐᒥ ᐊᑎᑎᒐᒍ -- ᐃᒡ
ᖃᑐᐊᕐᑦᑕᑐ ᑕᐊᑦᓚᓂ ᕐᔭᕐᐅᑦᑕᐅᕐᒪᓚᒥ ᐊᒻᓗ ᐊᕐᐊᕐᖅᖅ
ᖃᑐᐊᕐᒥᓂ. ᑲᑲᑐᐱᑕ ᑭᓇᐅᑦᑕᐅᕐᐊᖅᑲᕐᒪᕐᖅ ᖃᑐᐊᕐᒥᓇ.
ᓇᕐᕿ ᒻᕐᕐᑐᖅ ᑎᑎᑐᖅᕐᓂᓂ ᖃᐅᐱᕐᑐᓂ ᐊᒻᓗ ᑯᕌᕐᖅ
ᑐᑎᑭᕐ ᓇᐅᒻᖃᐊᕐ ᖃᐊᕐᕌᕐᕿ ᐃᒐᓂᕐ. ᐃᒡ ᑲᑲ ᑭᑐᒪᑦᓚ
ᐱᕐᐊᕐᕐᓄᕐ. ᐊᑕᐅᕐᐊᕐᑎ, ᑭᑐᒪᑦ ᓗ ᓇᕐᕿᐅᕐᓗ ᐅᐱᒪ,
ᐃᕐᕐᓚᓗ, ᐊᐅᑐᕐᐊᑕᐅᕐᒪᕌ ᖃᑐᐊᕐᑕᐊᐅᑐᕐᑎ ᑕᑯᕐᐊᑐᕐᕿᒍ
ᑐᐊᕐᒪᕐᖅ ᐊᑕᐅᐊᓗᕐᒥ. ᐊᕐᒥ ᕐᕐᐸᑕᐅᕐᑦ ᑕᐊᒪᐃᑎᑐᐅᕐᒪᕐᕐᕐᑦ.
ᐃᑕ ᐃᖃᓄᑕᐅᕐᕿᑐᐱᑦ ᑕᑯᕐᕿᑐᕐᒍ ᑕᐊᒪᒪ ᑎᕐᑎᓂᒍ ᒪᓇ
ᐅᕐᐸᕐᖅ ᑕᑯᕐᕿᒪᑭᕐᒪᕐᖅ.

ᑲᐅᕐᒪᕌ ᐊᕐᐅᕐᕐᑐᕐᖅ ᐃᓂᕐᑲᑎᐊᕐᖅ, ᐃᓂᑐᐃᓂᐅᕐᕿ
ᕐᕐᒥ ᑐᐃᕐ ᐊᒻᓗ ᐃᓂᕐᒪ ᑐᕐᑲᑎᕐᒪ ᓇᐃᑐᕐᕿ ᒪᓗ ᐊᑐᓂ
ᓄᓇᕐᒪᓄᐊᕐᒥ ᑕᑭᒍ. ᓄᑎᕐ ᐱᕐᐊᕐᒪᕐᕐᑐᕐᐅᒪ ᐃᓄᓪ ᑳᓇ

Caribou and birds.
Stone cut, 1963

ᐅᖃᓕᒫᕆ ᐊᒡᓗ ᑯᓚᕐᐊᑭ
ᐅᕐᑕᒥ ᑎᑎᑐᒪ, 1963

The knives, the drying rack,
the things we made to use.
Felt pen, 1970

ᓴᐱᑦ, ᐸᓂᐱᐊᑭ, ᓴᓚᕈᑲᑐᑐᑦ ᐊᑐ
ᓂᐊᑐᒥ ᐊᓚᒐᒐ ᐊᕿᐱᐅᒐ ᑎᑎᑐᒪ,
1970

after the white people's war, when the white men began to make many houses in the Arctic. Eskimos began to move into the settlements and then the white people started helping us to get these houses. That's why life changed. I don't think everybody was too fond of moving from the camps, but they still came anyway. Now they just stay here in Cape Dorset. They are working for the white man now.

Kaka didn't want to move away from his camp so now his camp has a real house. He had it moved down the shore.

In some ways I like living in a warm house, but in the old days, before all these things happened, we were always healthy. I was never sick, not even with all the children I had. In these late years I have been sick most of the time and I have felt each year harder to bear. Now that we all live in one place we get sick a lot. My worry now is over one of my sons who was very sick in the spring. He is down south now and I do not know how he is doing.

ᐅᓇᑎᖕᕈᓚᑎᓲᕆ, ᑲᔪᐊ ᐊᒥᕈᓂ ᐊᑭ ᔪᓴᐅᑎᐊᕐᓚᑕᐅᕐᓚᕐᑦ ᐊᓄᐊᑦ ᓄᐊᓚᓂ. ᐊᓄᐊᑦ ᓄᕐᑲᑎᓐᐊᕐᓚᕐᓚᕐ ᐊᑭᔪᑲᑐᒐᑦ ᐊᒡᓗ ᑕᐱᒪ ᑲᔪᐊᑦ ᐊᑭᑲᑎᐊᕐᓚᕐᓚᕐᑦ ᐅᐸᓂ ᑕᑯᒪ ᐊᑭᔪᑲᕐᐊᓯᑎᑦ. ᑕᐱᐊᒪ ᐊᓄᕐ ᐊᕐᕈᓚᑎᐅᑦ. ᐊᓄᓚᕐ ᓇᑐᓚᕐᐊᑭᐅᕐᑭᐅ ᓂᕐᐊᑭ ᓄᐊᓂ, ᐊᑎ ᓐᐱᑐᐊᓄᑐᐊᑦ. ᓚᓐᑦ ᑕᓚᐅᐊᓄᑐ ᐱᓂ. ᐊᑲᓇᐊᔭᐱᐊᑐ ᑲᔪᐊᓂ ᓚᓂ.

ᑲᑲ ᓄᔪᓚᑐᐱᑐ ᓄᐊᓂ ᑕᐱᒪ ᓚᓇ ᓄᐊᓚ ᐊᓄᓄᑐᑲᓐᑦ. ᑲᑲᐅᕐ ᓄᑐᐅᐱᐊᓐᑐᐅᑕᓄᕐ ᕐᔭᐅᑦ.

ᐊᑎᓚᔪᑦ ᐃᐱᔪᑐᓚ ᐅᑯᐅᒐᕐᒐᕐᑲ ᐊᑭ ᔪᕐ ᐊᑎ ᐅᑭᕐᐊᕈ ᑕᓚᑐᒐᑦ ᐊᑐᐊᑐᓂᕐᕆ, ᑕᐱᓚᑎᓐᕐ ᑲᓄᐊᐸᐊᐅᕐᒐᕐᕈᐊᑐᐅᕐ, ᑲᓄᓚᐊᑐᐅᑎᐊᑦ, ᑕᑯᓚᓐᓚᓴᐊᔪᓐ ᐱᑐᑲᐊᕐᕆᓪ. ᐊᓴᔪᑦ ᐅᑐ ᑲᓄᓚᐊᓄᓚᑐᐊᑐ ᐊᒡᓗ ᐊᓴᔪᑕᓚᑕ ᑲᓄᓚᐅᑎᕐᔭᐱᕐᕆᓪ. ᓚᓇ ᐊᔪᐊᑦ ᐊᑐᐅᔪᓚᓚᕐᑦ ᑲᓄᓚᔪᐊᕐᓚᓪᐊᐅᑐᔪ. ᐊᕐᒐᓐᑭᒐᕐᑲᓪ ᓚᓇ ᐊᔪᑐᔪᕐᓚᓐᓂᑦ ᐊᑭᓂᓚ ᐊᑎ ᑲᓄᓚᕐᓐᓚᐊᔪᓂᐅᑐᓪ ᐅᐱ ᕐᑲᓪ. ᑲᔪᐊ ᓄᐊᓚᓂᑐᔪ ᓚᓇ ᑲᑐᐱᒐᕐᓐᑐᓪ ᑲᓄᐊᓴᓐᓪᓪᑦ.

The little owl.
Stone cut, 1968

ᐅᑲ ᐱᐊᐱᑲ
ᐅᖕᕵᒥ ᑎᑎᑐᒪ, 1968

Fishing in front of the snow shelter.
Felt pen, ca. 1967

ᓱᒡᒥ ᐊᐳᒐᑐᖕᑲ ᐊᐳᑎᒥᑲ ᐅᒡᐊᑲᓂᒍ
ᐃᒪᒍ ᐊᖃᐳᑎᒍ ᑎᑎᑐᒪ,
1967 ᐅᑎᒍᒍ

A few years ago, too, there was a great loss in our family. Nawpachee and her husband, Eegyvudluk, were at church and they left their young children at home. The house caught fire and they died.

But I think the new ways would be better than the old, except that nowadays the young people make so much trouble. A long time ago when I was bringing up my children they would do what you told them to do. If you gave them something to eat they were grateful and happy about it. Ottochie, especially, was always thankful for everything. If he asked to do something and I said yes, he'd be really pleased; if I said no, he wouldn't do it. Now, all that has changed. They don't listen at all. People get worse when they all live in one place. The young people are always in trouble; if they were out of trouble, it would be much better the new way.

I have heard there is someone – not a human being but a spirit – in the moon. When I heard that the two men had

ᐊᒪᔪᑕ ᐅᑭᑕ ᐊᒥᕐᓱᑐ ᐊᓂᒍᑊᓕᓴᑐ ᐃᓴᐊᑐᐸᓲᓴᑐᔪᓯ
ᓇᐸᔪ ᐅᐊᒪᔪ, ᐊᕿᓴᐊᔪ ᑐᕐᐊᓴᑲᐊᕐᓱᑎ ᐱᐊᕐᒥᓂ ᑭᓚᐊᕿᓴ
ᓂᓯ ᑉᑊᐳᓗ ᕈᓂᓂᓗ, ᒡᓚᓄᑐᕐᓯᓚᒥ ᐃᓴᓯᕐᓂ ᑭᓗᓂ,
ᒡᓂᖁᓂ. ᐃᑊ ᓗ ᐃᒡᒡᓂᓚ ᑕᐊᒪ ᑕᒡᒡ ᑐᓗᓂᓂᕐᕈᑊ.

ᐃᓴ ᓂᑕᑊᑐᔪᓯ ᐱᐊᐅᑭᐊᕐᑊᒍ ᐅᕐᕐᒡᓂᑊᒥᒡᑊ, ᑭᕐᒡᓂ
ᓚᐳᓲ ᐅᐱᑊᐊᓯ ᒡᑊᕐᒡᓗ ᐱᓚᑊ(ᓪᓪᓯ). ᐅᕐᕐᒡᓂᒡᑊ
ᐱᒡᒡᑊ ᐱᒡᒡᐳᑎᓗᕐ ᒡᓯᕐᒡ(ᑊᓪᓪ) ᐅᑊᑊᐅᑎᑭ. ᒡᒡᑐᑭᒍ
ᕈᓂᒍᐃᓚᒥ ᓂᑎᓚᕐᒥ ᓂᑲᕐᒡᕿᑐᓴ) ᒡᓴᒡᕐᕈᕐᓗ. ᐅᑊᑐᑭ,
ᐱᒍᒡᑎᓂᒍ. ᑕᒡᒪᒪ ᓯᑎᕿ ᕿᓂᓯᒥ. ᕈᓂᒡᐃᓚᓂᒍᓚᕐᒥ
ᒡᐱᑎᓴᒡᓪᓯ ᑕᒡᒪ, ᒡᕐᒡᒍ, ᒡᑊᕐᒡᓲᑊ ᒡᔪᒡᕿᕐᕿᑭᓴ)ᑊ;
ᒡᕐᕐᑎᒡᒪᒪ, ᑊᓗᓂᐅᕐᓗᒥᓂ. ᓚᓯᒡ ᐃᓲᓂᑎ ᑕᐊᓚᐊᔪᓂᐊᕐ.
ᓂᑎᕐᕿᒡᓯ. ᐃᓂᐊ ᐱᕈᒡᕐᒡᓴᓯᓂ ᐃᓲᓂᑎ ᒡᑕᐳᕐᕿᐊᓂᒥ
ᓂᓂᑊᓪᓯᒡᑊᓗᒥ. ᐅᐱᑊᐃ ᑕᒡᒪᑊᒡᒪ ᐱᐊᓯᑊᕈ ᐱᓚᑊᑊᓯᕐᑊᕐᕈ
ᐱᐊᕐᕿᕐᓲᒍᓯᕐᔪᕐ ᓂᑊᔪᓗᓂ ᐱᐅᕐᑊ.

ᑐᕿᕐᓚᕐᕈ ᑭᓂᒍᐃᓂᑊᑎᕐ ᐃᓴᓂᑎ ᐃᓴ ᑐᓗ -- ᑕᑊᕐᑎᕐᑊ.
ᑐᕿᕐᒡ ᒡᒍᓂᑊ ᓗᑐ ᓂᓂᒡᓲᓂᕐᔪᒡᕐ ᑕᑭᕐᒍ. ᐊᕐᒡᕐᒡᕿᒪ

In summer we hunted dulse
on the beach.
Felt pen, ca. 1967

ᐊᐅᔭᒥ ᑭᒡᐊᔪᐅᐸᓪᒪᑐᒍ ᓲᔅᒥ
ᐃᒪᓪᒍ ᐊᓕᐅᑎᒍ ᑎᑎᑐᒪ,
I 967 ᐅᑎᓲᒍ

Fishing through the ice.
Coloured pencil and felt pen,
ca. 1967

ᓲᒍᒥ ᐊᐅᓴᓴᑐᖕ
ᑲᖕᓴᓓ ᐊᓕᐅᑎ ᐊᒪᓗ ᐃᒪᓕᒍᓱᒎ
ᑎᑎᑐᒪ, I 967 ᐅᑎᓲᒍ

Spirit of happy women.
Coloured pencil and felt pen,
ca. 1967

ᐊᒃ ᓇᐅᑉ ᑯᕕᐊᓯᓂᒐ
ᑕᒃ ᓴᓚᖕ ᐊᓚᐅᑎᖕ ᐊᒪᖕ ᐃᒪᓚᒧᑦ
ᑎᑎᑐᒐ, 1967 ᐅᑎᖕᒍ

landed on the moon I wondered what the spirit thought of these two men landing on his land.

ᑲᖕ ᑐᒐᒃ ᐃᓯᒪᓂᒪᒐᑦ ᑕᑯᓂᒐ ᐊᒍᑎᓂ ᒪᕆᓂ ᖕᓇᑐᓂᒃ, ᖕᓇᒐᖕᑦ.

We have an Anglican church here in Cape Dorset and every Sunday I go there. The missionaries came to the Arctic a long time ago and I was married by the Anglican clergyman, Inutaquuq. But for a long time we had no church in Cape Dorset. Then Pootagook, the father of Eegyvudluk, Nawpachee's husband, told the missionaries that they should bring a church to Cape Dorset. He said the Eskimos would give fox skins to pay for materials.

ᑐᓯᐊᕕᑲᑐᒍᑦ ᐊᔪᑭᑐᐃᕗᑯᑦ ᑐᓯᐊᕕᒐᓂ ᒪᓂ ᑭᒐᓂ ᐊᒪᖕ ᐊᓚᖠᐊᑕᒪ ᑕᐃᑯᒐᐸᑐᒐ. ᐊᔪᑭᑐᐃᕗ ᐃᖕᐃ ᖕᓇᒐᖕᓚᐅᓯᒪᔪ ᐅᕿᓯᐊᕆᐊᖕ ᐊᒪᖕ ᑲᑎᑎᑕᐅᓯᒪᔪᒐ ᐊᔪᑭᑐᐃᕗᒧ ᐃᖕᑕᒍᒧ. ᐃᓚ ᐅᕿᓯᐊᕆᓂᓂᐊᖕ ᑐᓯᐊᕕᑲᓚᐅᕆᑐᒍ ᑭᒐᓂ. ᑕᐃᒪ ᐳᑐᒍ ᐃᕿᖕᐊᔪᑉ ᐊᑕᑕᒐ, ᓇᐸᓯᐅᖕ ᐅᐃᒐ, ᐅᑲᐅᑎᓚᐅᓯᒪᔪᒃ ᐊᔪᑭᑐᐃᕗᓂᒃ ᑐᓯᐊᕕᑕᑲᐃᔪᓴᐅᕆᐊᕆᓂ ᑭᒐᓂ. ᐅᑲᓚᐅᓯᒪᔪ ᐃᖕᐃ ᑐᓂᓯᑲᑕᓂᐊᒪᑕ ᑎᖠᒐᓂᐊᔭᓂ ᐊᑭᓕᒍᑎᓴᓂ ᑐᓯᐊᕕᓴᒍᑦ.

The missionaries brought it and Pootagook had them put it over at the end of the bay where the children wouldn't get at it. He told them to put it there. Pootagook and other Eskimos led the services but, later, a clergyman came and lived here for a time. The women in Cape Dorset sewed sealskin cushions and we also embroidered hangings for the altar. Many women embroidered birds and seals and other animals in bright colours on small

ᐊᔪᑭᑐᐃᕗᐅᑉ ᓂᐅᕕᐊᖠᓚᐅᓯᒪᔭᒐ ᑕᐃᒪ ᐳᑐᓚᐅᑉ ᐃᓚᕗᑯᓚ ᐅᓯᒪᔭᕆ ᐃᒪᐅᑉ ᐃᓯᐊᖕ ᑕᐃᑲᓂ ᐱᐊᕋᖕ ᐅᐃᕕᓴᑕᐅᓂᐊᕆᒪ ᐅᑲᐅᑎᓚᐅᓯᒪᔭᕆ ᑕᐃᑯᒐᑕᐅᑯᓯᒍ. ᐳᑐᓚ ᐊᓯᕆᖕ ᐃᖕᐃᑦ ᑐᓯᐊᑎᓯᕗᐅᕿᓚᐅᑐ ᐃᓚ ᓯᐊᕆ ᐊᔪᑭᑐᐃᕗ ᑎᑭᓚᐅᓯᓇᔪᒃ ᑕᒪᓂᓚᑐ ᐊᑯᓂᐊᖕ. ᐊᒃ ᓇᐃᑦ ᑭᒐᒥᐅ ᒥᓯᓚᐅᓯᒪᔪ ᓇᓯᐅᑉ ᑭᓯᕆᓂ ᐊᑎᑎᓂ ᑕᐃᒪᖕᑕᐅ ᑕᓯᑐᐃᓚᐅᓯᒪᒥᔪᒍ ᑲᒐᑕᔪᓴᓂ ᑐᓯᐊᕕᐅᑉ ᐃᒥᕕᒐᓂ. ᐊᒥᓯᑦ ᐊᒃ ᓇᐃᑦ ᑕᒃ ᓴᓚᐅᓚᐅᓯᒪᔪᑦ ᑯᐸᖕᐊᒍᐊᓂ ᐊᒪᖕ ᓇᓯᒍᐊᓂ ᐊᓯᕆᓂᖕ ᐅᒪᔪᓂ ᓂᑕᓚᖠᑎᖕᕆ

Waiting.
Felt pen, 1970

The old life was hard – but it was happy.
Felt pen, ca. 1967

ᐅᑕᑭᔭᒃ
ᐃᒪᓕᒧ ᐊᓚᐅᑎᒧᑦ ᑎᑎᑐᒐ, 1970

ᐃᓄᓯᑐᑲ ᐊᓯᕆᓇᕆᓗᐊᓯᓂ ᑯᕕᐊᓇᐸᓚᐅ
ᑐᒃ ᐃᒪᓕᒧᑦ ᑎᑎᑐᒐ,
1967 ᐅᑎᓗᒍ

squares of cloth. But we did much more embroidery than is there in the church today. What happened to it? Well, we think one of the missionaries' wives stole some of it. When all the squares were sewn together they looked very nice.

I have heard that they like my drawings in the south and I am grateful and happy about it. Nowadays, when very special people arrive on the plane to visit the Co-op, I am always invited. I am usually very shy but often they shake hands. Last week a very important minister was here from Ottawa and they gave him the stone which was made from one of my drawings. It was a sealskin boat I did last winter.

To make prints is not easy. You must think first and this is hard to do. But I am happy doing the prints. After my husband died I felt very alone and unwanted; making prints is what has made me happiest since he died. I am going to keep on doing them until they tell me to stop. If no

ᑕᒃᓴᒥ ᒥᑭᔭᑎᓂ ᓯᓂᕆᑐᒍᓯᑎ ᑲᓗᓇᑕᓂ. ᐃᓚ ᐊᒥᓯᑲᓂᓂᒃ ᑕᒃᓯᑐᐃᓚᐅᓯᒪᑎᓗᑕ ᐱᑕᑲᓯᐊᒍᓇᐃᑐ ᑐᓯᐊᕕᒥ ᒪᓇ. ᑲᓄᐃ ᓕᓂᑲ? ᑕᒐ ᐊᔭᑭᑐᐃᔪ ᐃᓚᒐᑕ ᓄᓕᐊᒐᓄ ᑎᓕᒐᕕᓂᐅᔭᑎᔪᕗ ᐃᓚᒥᑦ. ᐃᓗᓇᑎ ᓯᓂᕆᑐ ᒥᓯᓯᒪᓕᑐᐊᒐᒥᒃ ᑲᑎᒪᓯᑎᒃ ᐱᐅᔭᐸᓗᓚᐅᓯᒪᔭᑦ.

ᑐᓴᓚᐅᑐᒐ ᑎᑎᑐᔪᒐᑲ ᐱᐅᒋᔪᐅᒋᐊᒋᑦ ᑲᓗᓇᑦ ᓄᓇᒐᓂ, ᓇᑯᓴᑐᒐ ᑯᕕᐊᓯᒐᓗ ᑕᑯᐊ ᒥᓴᓄ. ᒪᓇᐅᓕᑐ, ᐊᒐᔭᑲᒪᑎᒃ ᑎᑭᒪᑕ ᑲᒐᑕᓯᑯ ᓂᐅᕆᓯᑎ ᑯᐅᐊᐸᒧ, ᑲᐃᑯᔪᐅᒋᓇᓯᒍᔭᒐ ᐊᒃᓯᐊᓗ ᑲᒍᓯᓯᒍᔭᒐ ᐃᓚ ᓴᐃᒧᐸᑐᒍ. ᐱᓇᓯᐊᕆᓯᐅᓚᐅᑐᒥ ᐊᒐᔭᑲᒪᑎ ᑕᒪᓂᓚᐅᒪᑦ ᐊᑐᒐᒥ ᐱᓯᓂ ᑕᐃᒪ ᐅᔪᕋᒥᒃ ᐊᐃᑐᑕᐅᓚᐅᑐᒃ ᐊᑭᓯᑕᕕᓂᒥ ᑎᑎᑐᔪᒪ ᐃᓚᒐᓂ. ᓇᓯᐅᑉ ᑭᓯᒋᓚᐅᑕᒐ ᐅᒥᐊ ᑎᑎᑐᔪᓚᐅᑕᒐ ᐊᕋᓂ.

ᑎᑎᑐᔪᑎᐊᓴ ᐱᑐᐃᓇᐅᒋᑐ. ᐃᓯᒪᒋᐊᑲᓇᑐ ᐊᒪᓗ ᑕᓇ ᑕᕙ ᐱᔪᑎᐊᑐᔭᐸᓗ. ᐃᓚ ᑯᕕᐊᓯᑐᒐ ᑎᑎᑐᔪᓕᐅᑎᐊᓴᒃ. ᐅᐃᒐ ᑐᑯᒐᓕᑎᓗᒍ ᐃᑭᐊᑐᐸᓗᓚᐅᒐᒪ ᐃᓄᑐᐊᒍᓯᒐᓗ, ᑎᑎᑐᔪᓕᐅᓯᒐ ᑯᕕᐊᓯᑎᑕᐅᓂᐸᐅᓯᒪᔭᒐ ᑕᐃᒪᒐᓂ ᐅᐃᒐ ᑐᑯᓚᐅᓯᒪᒪ.

one tells me to stop, I shall make them as long as I am well.
If I can, I'll make them even after I am dead.

My son, Kumwartok, wants me to do some drawings to put
around the house. But I think I will probably do some and
take them to the Co-op.

ᑎᑎᑐᕐᒥᓕᑲᓕ ᖅᐊᐅᕐᒥᓕ ᐸᑐᐃᓇᒍ ᓇ ᖅᐊᐅᕐ ᐅᕐᑯᒪ, ᑎᑎᑐᕐ ᐃᓇᓕᑲᓕ ᖃᐃᕐᒥᓕ. ᒍᓇᒪᒪ.

ᐃᖃᓇ ᒍᓕᐊ ᑎᑎᑐᕐᑯᖕᐊᐅᑐ ᐅᖕᓇ ᐃᒍᑎᓇ ᖃᓇᐸᒪᖃᓇ. ᐃᓇ ᑎᑎᑐᕐᑐᒍᑐᒪ ᑎᑎᑐᕐᑕᖃ ᒍᐅᐊᔪᑐ ᐃᓇᓕᒍᑎᕐ.